To the memory of Immanuel Wallerstein,
who started crying 'Wolf!' thirty years ago,
falling mostly on deaf ears.

THE END OF TRUTH

FIVE ESSAYS ON THE DEMISE OF NEOLIBERALISM

THE END OF TRUTH

FIVE ESSAYS ON THE DEMISE OF NEOLIBERALISM

Bülent Somay

TRANSNATIONAL PRESS LONDON

2021

SOCIETY AND POLITICS: 6

THE END OF TRUTH - FIVE ESSAYS ON THE DEMISE OF
NEOLIBERALISM

Bülent Somay

Copyright © 2021 Transnational Press London

First Published in 2021 by Transnational Press London in the United Kingdom, 13 Stamford Place, Sale, M33 3BT, UK.
www.tplondon.com

Transnational Press London® and the logo and its affiliated brands are registered trademarks.

Requests for permission to reproduce material from this work should be sent to:
sales@tplondon.com

Paperback
ISBN: 978-1-912997-87-9
Digital
ISBN: 978-1-80135-027-3

Cover Design: Nihal Yazgan
Cover Photo by Joël de Vriend on Unsplash.com

‘On Radical Ambiguity’ was originally written in English and published in Turkish translation in Çokbilmiş Özne (The Subject who Knows Too Much, ©Metis Publishers, Istanbul, 2008). It is used here by permission from the publishers.

‘The Midas Blessing: Turning Commodities into Gifts’ was first published as a chapter in the book Yesterday's Tomorrows: On Utopia and Dystopia, eds. Pere Gallardo and Elizabeth Russell, ©Cambridge Scholars, Tyne, 2014. It is used here by permission from the publishers.

Transnational Press London Ltd. is a company registered in England and Wales No. 8771684

CONTENTS

ABOUT THE AUTHOR

Bülent Somay is born in Istanbul and had his BA and MA degrees in English Language and Literature, and PhD degree in Psychosocial Studies. He was a Lecturer in Comparative Literature and Cultural Studies in Istanbul Bilgi University between 2000 and 2017. He has published seven books in Turkish (*Cinselliğe Dair Vazgeçmemiz Gereken Yüz Efsane* [A Hundred Myths on Sexuality We Need to Give Up], 2016; *Tarih, Otobiyografi ve Hakikat* [History, Autobiography and Truth], 2015, ed.; *Çokbilmiş Özne* [The Subject Who Knows Too Much], 2008; *Bir Şeyler Eksik* [Something is Missing], 2007; *Tarihin Bilinçdışı* [The Unconscious of History], 2004; *Şarkı Okuma Kitabı* [Song Reader], 2000; *Geriye Kalan Devrimdir* [What Remains is the Revolution], 1997), and two books in English (*The View from the Masthead*, 2010; *The Psychopolitics of the Oriental Father*, 2014). His most recent publication is Something is *Missing: Things We don't Want to Know about Love, Sex and Life*, published by Transnational Press, London, 2021. He is recently living in exile as an Academy in Exile fellow in Freie Universität, Berlin.

PREFACE

The five essays in this book were written in different times and circumstances, some of them against very dissimilar backdrops. The older ones, however, were massively rewritten and updated during the course of 2020 in Berlin, through the *Weltschmerz* of the Covid-19 crisis, under sometimes voluntary and sometimes compulsory lockdown.

The first ('On Radical Ambiguity') was originally written in English in 2007, and published in Turkish translation in my book *Çokbilmiş Özne* (The Subject who Knows Too Much, ©Metis Publishers, Istanbul, 2008). It is used here by permission from the publishers. For this edition I expanded and significantly updated the English original which was never published before, considering that the years in between constituted maybe one of the most eventful decades in recent history. My thanks are for my translator (from English to Turkish) in 2007, Didem Kizen, and my editor (again in 2007) Müge Gürsoy Sökmen, whose rendition and comments back then helped me a lot when I sat down to update the essay in 2020.

The second, ('The Midas Blessing: Turning Commodities into Gifts') was first presented as a paper in the 13th International Conference of Utopian Studies, held in Tarragona, Spain, in 2012, and later published as a chapter in the book *Yesterday's Tomorrows: On Utopia and Dystopia*, eds. Pere Gallardo and Elizabeth Russell (©Cambridge Scholars, Tyne, 2014). It is used here by permission from the publishers. It is likewise much expanded and updated, since its subject matter, digital reproduction and intellectual property, is one of the most rapidly evolving and deeply controversial areas in intellectual and artistic endeavour and related copyright- and patent-dependent sectors.

The third essay ('The End of Truth as We Know It: The Disintegration of University Discourse') was one of the outcomes of a project I started at the University of Oslo, where I spent a year (2018-19) on a Scholars at Risk scholarship, and continued at Freie Universität, Berlin as an Academy in Exile fellow (2019-21). I thank Steffen Krüger in the UiO, who was my only reader and critic in Oslo, 2019, and Ozan Zeybek, who did the same in Berlin, 2020. Julia Strutz in Off-University, Berlin, was always there with much needed encouragement when I was trying to make heads or tails with many issues in the effort to 'Re-think and Re-imagine University'.

The fourth and fifth essays ('*The Game of Thrones* as a Failed Attempt at Universal Populism' and 'The Psychopolitics of the Entitled Victim: The Coming of Age of Contemporary Populism'), as well as the Introduction, were also written in 2020 in Berlin, for which a vote of thanks is due to the Academy in Exile. I also thank Ömer Turan, whose criticism and comments from afar made the very lonely process of writing (in 2020) a little more bearable.

And finally, I thank my comrade and partner, Ezgi Keskinsoy, *sine qua non*, who was there in every step of the way, my fiercest critic and most meticulous editor. As usual, she changed the course of my writing many times, and defeated my stubborn self-defence in each case with persistent calm.

INTRODUCTION: AFTER NEOLIBERALISM, THE FLOOD?

> So, what is this neo-liberalism? […] The problem of neo-liberalism is rather how the overall exercise of political power can be modelled on the principles of a market economy. […]
>
> So, it is a matter of a market economy without *laissez-faire*, that is to say, an active policy without state control. Neoliberalism should not therefore be identified with *laissez-faire*, but rather with permanent vigilance, activity, and intervention.
>
> Foucault, *The Birth of Biopolitics* (2008 [1978-79]), 131-2

> 'Let's be clear about what's going on,' Deran Wu said. 'It's the end of civilization as we know it. And it's going to be great for business.'
>
> John Scalzi, *The Last Emperox* (2020)

There is little doubt that when the history of the first half of the 21st century is written, historians will endlessly argue over whether the 'Golden Shot' of the Covid-19 Pandemic was really necessary to sound the death-knell of liberal/neoliberal capitalism. Even the late Immanuel Wallerstein, who correctly predicted the end of liberalism (and consequently its 'new and improved version', neoliberalism), insistently written about it since 1992 (Wallerstein 1992, 1995, 1999), and even more correctly placed the critical moment of this downfall somewhere around 2020, could not have foreseen that the Grim Reaper who came for liberalism/neoliberalism would wear a crown.

To be sure, this by no means indicates that neoliberal capitalism will docilely go away on its own accord and leave its place to a freer and more egalitarian system, Covid-19 or not. Wallerstein had already commented on the open-endedness of the projected demise of 'liberalism' in 1995:

> [I]t is by no means assured that the end of one inegalitarian historical system will result in a better one. The struggle is quite open. We need today to define the concrete institutions through which human liberation can finally be expressed. We have lived through its pretended expression in our existing world-system, in which liberal ideology tried to persuade us of a reality that the liberals were in fact struggling against—the reality of increasing equality and democracy. And we have lived through the disillusionment of failed antisystemic movements, movements that were themselves part of the problem as much as they were a part of the solution (Wallerstein 1995, 144).

Philosophers and thinkers who look forward to the end of capitalism with varying degrees of eagerness, cannot agree upon the character of the aftermath: Giorgio Agamben, for instance (Agamben 2020), predicts with regard to the Covid-19 crisis (to the chagrin of his friend Jean-Luc Nancy), an even more inegalitarian system, using the existing 'state of exception' for a more strict and permanent surveillance society, while Slavoj Žižek (Žižek 2020) sounds more optimistic, expecting a more communitarian outcome, albeit not much more libertarian.[1]

Each thinker regards the Covid-19 crisis with reference to their trademark concepts, and comes up with a slightly different (or seemingly *entirely* different) conception of the near future. It is possible to say that each of them, just like in the parable of the elephant and the blind men,[2] sees (or, metaphorically, *touches*) and points out a part of the truth, and their interpretations should be considered together to arrive at a more or less comprehensive whole, rather than as conflicting claims. Despite the visible differences in interpretation and expectation, however, they all converge, whether implicitly or explicitly, in the understanding that the Covid-19 crisis is not merely a 'natural disaster' as such, a solitary RNA molecule challenging civilisation as we know it, but rather a part of a contingency, meeting and converging with the imminent and immanent crisis of neoliberal capitalism, and making it visible to the naked eye. There are six main points we can designate on how the Covid-19 managed to do this:

- It unveiled the profoundly inadequate system of healthcare devised by neoliberal capitalism, not only in 'underdeveloped' or 'developing' countries at the fringes of the capitalist world-system, but also at its very core, especially in the US and the UK. The inadequacy of this system consisted of (a) the very fragile network of health protection for the working class and the middle classes which fell apart at the first serious blow; (b) the immense power of the pharmacological industry built entirely upon profit maximisation and considered people with ailments and disabilities as nothing but clients; and (c) the equally immense power of the insurance sector which profited by keeping a significant part of the population un- or under-insured, making the 'service' they sell

---

[1] Here is a more or less comprehensive compilation of the initial argument around the Covid-19 pandemic, in *European Journal of Psychoanalysis*: https://www.journal-psychoanalysis.eu/coronavirus-and-philosophers/. Žižek, on the other hand, was quick to publish an entire book about it in April, and a second one in November (Žižek1 2020; Žižek2 2020). See also blog entries by Joseph Owen (https://www.versobooks.com/blogs/4636-states-of-emergency-metaphors-of-virus-and-covid-19) and by Judith Butler (https://www.versobooks.com/blogs/4603-capitalism-has-its-limits) in Verso website.

[2] The original (or earliest) version of this parable is to be found in a Buddhist text (*Udana* 6.4) ca. 500 BC, and the most comprehensive version is in Rumi's *Masnavi* (Book III, Story V) in the 13th Century, although it is known in the English-speaking world in its 19th century version by the American poet John Godfrey Saxe.

a scarce commodity, and also by keeping as many diseases and disabilities untreated as it could.

- It acted as a harbinger for and dress rehearsal of what is likely to happen if and when the environmental disaster predicted by almost all responsible and knowledgeable scientists hits the globe with full-force. Neoliberal capitalism has proven not only totally unprepared for such a practically inevitable encounter, but also that it has systematically dismantled almost all possible physical and psychological measures against it beforehand, as 'detrimental' to the profitable functioning of the capitalist world-system.

- It not only exposed the extreme vulnerability of the neoliberal system to economic recession and unemployment, but also shattered the seemingly self-evident separation between essential vs. unessential work and between productive vs. unproductive labour, thereby inviting scrutiny on the entire 'rational' foundation of the capitalist mode of production. It also made possible an inevitable inquiry on the split between production for human wants/needs vs. production for profit, and ultimately invalidated the liberal and neoliberal arguments that these two are indeed one and the same.

- It made visible how fragile and shaky the existing regime of Truth had become, having already been replaced with a series of negotiations, approximations and concessions which made discerning truths from non-truths and lies, and fact from fiction almost impossible. The demarcation line between information and knowledge had already been challenged by the ascendancy of the World Wide Web, and at the same time by the categorical equalisation of all methodological/rational processing of information with simple statements of non-truths and lies.

- It uncovered the profound disintegration of university discourse by an out-and-out commodification of the production, transmission and dissemination of knowledge. The seemingly universal accessibility of higher education, and equally universal inaccessibility of its products by an over-sophistication of the language of knowledge, as well as the monopolised control over academic publishing, collapsed due to the necessity of so-called 'social distancing' and the consequent migration to online methods and venues, and started to threaten the already precarised academic professions.

- It illuminated the interactions, overlaps and coincidences between class struggle, women's liberation movement(s), LGBTI+ liberation movement(s) and ethnic liberation movement(s). It created a historic moment where all of these escalated and intensified at precisely the same time with no or little conflict between them, reducing most existing conflicts and discussions between them to mere rhetoric and *ressentiment*-driven brawls, where class struggle and movements giving priority to class-conflict no longer hindered but rather tended to consolidate and enhance anti-racist, anti-sexist and anti-homophobic/transphobic struggle(s).

It is, therefore, necessary to investigate the impending (or rather, already-arrived) crisis of neoliberalism, rather than the Covid-19 catastrophe itself, which is lurking around us while we helplessly try to ascribe meaning(s) to the ways it is substantially changing our lives. The 'crisis of neoliberalism', in turn, is not only a crisis of a specific phase (and/or ideology) of capitalism, but as a crisis indicating the demise of the Capitalist World-System as we know it, and also the demise of liberalism as a whole.

What is this Neoliberalism anyway?

This is almost the same question Foucault had asked as early as 1979 (see Foucault 2008, above), and answered quite comprehensively, so much so that after forty-one years there is little to add to his basic definition: Neoliberalism is more than a simple return to 'Trevelyanism'[3] after a longish hiatus, a return to unhindered 'free market' capitalism, but this time through state coercion (a perfect oxymoron if there is one), after the mostly unsuccessful regime of state intervention in the inner workings of capitalism supposedly in favour of the 'middle' and working classes ('Welfare State'), starting from the Great Depression, through the aftermath of the Second Great War and up to the '1968 revolution' (Wallerstein), after which the world-system reverts to the original structure it had assumed in the first half of the 19th century. In the same instance, Wallerstein labels neoliberalism a false name for resurgent conservatism (Wallerstein 1999, 43).

Neoliberalism, however, proved to be more than a mere 'false name' for conservatism, but conservatism with a renewed structure, not only a return to an unhindered market economy, but an attempt to overhaul and restructure society. According to Foucault, it is an attempt to reshape (late) capitalism not only on the economic level, but also in governmental and cultural spheres, and even in everyday life:

> Government must not form a counterpoint or a screen, as it were, between society and economic processes. It has to intervene on society as such, in its fabric and depth. Basically, it has to intervene on society so that

---

[3] Thankfully, such a thing as 'Trevelyanism' (as a name) never existed in actual history. Sir Charles Trevelyan was in charge of the relief effort in Ireland during the Potato Blight (1845-49), and his fanatic, almost religious belief in *laissez faire*, that the government should never interfere in the Free Market no matter what, even in order to save lives, was one of the reasons that about a million people died and two million immigrated out of Ireland. Compared to this, today's neoliberalism is, so to speak, 'Trevelyanism with a huge stick'.

competitive mechanisms can play a regulatory role at every moment and every point in society and by intervening in this way its objective will become possible, that is to say, a general regulation of society by the market. (Foucault 2008, 145)

'A general regulation of society by the market,' however, cannot function without corresponding 'micro practices of subjectification,' according to Ferda Keskin (Keskin 2016), who reads Foucault's commentary on neoliberalism as a reshaping of society, as a third phase in societal control mechanisms of capitalism, that of *Governmentality*, after Territorial Sovereignty and Discipline.[4] We must, then, attempt to make a short chronological review of how capitalism and liberalism appeared on the historical scene pretending to be 'two peas in a pod', how they got separated or severed, how neoliberalism emerged allegedly 'reuniting' these two by discarding everything even closely resembling freedom within liberalism, and finally, how it went into rapid decline with the profound crisis of capitalism, accompanied by a global security crisis.

A recent example may be of some help in understanding the underlying irresolvable problems of neoliberalism: As it came to pass, in the early days of 2021, some major Wall Street hedge funds have gambled on the fast and steady downfall of Gamestop shares, a gaming firm. A crowd organized through Reddit taking the same gamble better, starting early January 2021, caused these shares to *increase* in value by 1,700% by the last week of January. Hedge funds, which 'borrow' Gamestop shares, sell them (therefore causing them to fall more), buy them back cheaper as the stock devalues, and pay off their debts and make millions of dollars as they sit comfortably in their armchairs (which is called 'shorting' in Wall Street jargon), watched open-mouthed as their profits melted away and gradually turned into losses. Some of them even declared bankruptcy. Doleful wails rose from Wall Street to get the Government to 'ban' this practice. What was going to be banned? Let others, organized crowds, be banned from playing the same game they have been playing for a hundred years; that's what the Wall Street networks wanted. Those of us searching for a more precise definition of 'neoliberalism' may rejoice, because there is no better definition than this. Of course (in the long run) is it not really possible to beat Wall Street at its own game. Neoliberal capitalism is meant for situations just like this one. The state, or intermediary financial organisations which at first profited from this game of course stepped in and prevented the game from being disrupted, by bending the law, ignoring it if necessary, and resorting to

---

[4] Cf. Keskin 2016: Keskin suggests, taking his cue from Foucault's argument on neoliberalism, that capitalism has ruled in the West under three modalities of power: (i) Territorial sovereignty, where the security and sustainability of the ruler is paramount, and where power is exercised by dictating what not to do (prohibition) through law ; (ii) Discipline, where power is exercised by dictating what to do (imperative) through normation; and (iii) Governmentality, where the governed are involved in a complex network of regulatory procedures, not as mere, passive consent-givers, but as active economic subjects through practices of subjectification.

main force if necessary. The genie, however, is out of the bottle: we see every day the structural weaknesses of neoliberal capitalism, how it slowly comes apart at the seams. The revolution, of course, will not take place in the stock market, but we can also see in the stock market what can happen if the crowd comes together and acts together with a certain purpose.[5]

In the early days of capitalism, the liberalisation of the market and the libera(lisa)tion of the 'individual' allegedly went hand in hand, without much tension, because a supposedly 'free' market called for free individuals, free from state, religious, family and community pressures and limitations, in order to be able to compete with each other freely in the 'marketplace'. Their only bondage was supposed to be to the *market*, which was not a tangible master *per se*, so in these early phases, capitalism appeared as a liberator, since the new master was not easily discernible to the naked eye. In the much-quoted passage from the first chapter of the *Communist Manifesto*, Marx and Engels insistently emphasised this so-called 'liberating' aspect of early capitalism:

> The bourgeoisie, wherever it has got the upper hand, has put an end to all feudal, patriarchal, idyllic relations. [...] It has drowned the most heavenly ecstasies of religious fervour, of chivalrous enthusiasm, of philistine sentimentalism, in the icy water of egotistical calculation. It has resolved personal worth into exchange value, and in place of the numberless indefeasible chartered freedoms, has set up that single, unconscionable freedom— Free Trade. In one word, for exploitation, veiled by religious and political illusions, it has substituted naked, shameless, direct, brutal exploitation. (Marx & Engels 2010b, 486-7)

Although 'neoliberalism' was marketed as a return to these 'liberating', even revolutionary early days, it was exactly the opposite. There were three main reasons why, following the reconstruction after the Second Great War, the capitalist world-system sought to return to a 'golden age' (which, like all golden ages, never existed in reality), calling this effort 'neoliberalism', which was in fact neither 'new' nor 'liberal'.

In actuality, capitalism had never completely managed to wipe out 'all feudal, patriarchal, idyllic relations [...] the most heavenly ecstasies of religious fervour, of chivalrous enthusiasm, of philistine sentimentalism.' The passage in the Manifesto was more of an expression of a propensity, rather than a description of the actual situation in 1848. There was always a massive remainder, expressed in the wishful retrospective fantasies of the reactionaries, or in the unchanging beliefs and steadfast, antediluvian institutions of the

---

[5] A note for enthusiasts, by the way, and conversely for those who proudly say, 'I don't read science fiction!': What happened in the 'Gamestop Affair' was described almost *mot-a-mot* in the 1955 novel by Frederik Pohl and Cyril Kornbluth, *Gladiator-At-Law*. If we take SF a little more seriously, we can see what rich strategies and tactics can be found there, after weeding out the garbage, and be astounded.

conservatives. In every crisis capitalism faced, the ruling class resorted to the much older and more deep-rooted institutions and discourses of conservatism, and reactionary fantasies surfaced as a way out, as an agenda for reconstruction of the status quo ante (that is, ante-capitalism), which may very well be called 'retro-construction'.

Recurring crises had retained and replenished the adversarial/ revolutionary potential of the working class and the unrest of the constantly threatened, downsized and dispossessed rural and middle classes, which had to be contained by successive concessions, by improved healthcare and education prospects, by a slow but steady enhancement of wages, consumption and leisure time, and by improved representation and presence in the political sphere. Most of these concessions had clashed, sometimes violently, with the 'needs of the market' and 'free competition'; in other words, laissez faire increasingly came into conflict with laissez passer. The 'free market' had to be increasingly limited and crippled by the needs of a welfare state, which was necessary to keep the revolutionary/transforming (and sometimes reactionary, keeping in mind that this term frequently included the peasantry and the lumpenproletariat) potential of the working classes, and the (sometimes violently) reactionary urges of the middle classes under check.

Capitalism had always been a 'World-System' since its conception (Wallerstein 2004), but this was contingent on the definition of the term 'World'. The entire history of capitalism is also the history of this conceptual 'World' eventually expanding (both semantically and geographically) from 'Europe' to 'the Earth'. The extension of capitalism outside Europe commenced and sustained a lengthy and painful process of so-called 'modernisation' (read 'becoming capitalist') in Asia, Africa, Oceania and the Americas, and bourgeois society supposedly absorbed the pre-existing native populations, cultures and ancient civilisations alike, putatively re-designing them in its own likeness. The reality, however, was much grimmer than that: bourgeois society was neither inclusive nor subtle and versatile enough for such absorption, so it also changed itself with every coerced inclusion, and the more it 'modernised' other cultures and civilisations, the more amorphous and unstructured it became. After the two great global wars which pulled all the world 'together' towards the same destiny, and eventually, with the so-called 'globalisation' process, the liberal/capitalist edifice lost its structural integrity and started to split at the seams.

With the advent of so-called 'Globalisation', capitalism reached its natural borders, provided, of course, that no pre- or non-capitalist, not-yet-proletarianised populations existed elsewhere in the solar system. This meant, among other things, in the declining profitability crises yet to come, it would have no option but to turn on itself, in an act of self-cannibalism, and try to extract the needed surplus value *from within*, rather than exporting the problem to other zones around the world, parts not yet absorbed in the World-System. Because no such zones remained. That is to say, as the World-System became a 'World-System' not only conceptually but also literally, liberalism, both as the founding ideology and the basic structural pattern of capitalism, would have to be invented anew. This re-invention, however, came after two centuries of dealing with conservatism and reaction, after the hiatus of the 'Welfare State' of constant manipulation of the market by the state, and after the forcible inclusion of cultures and civilisations not fundamentally compatible with capitalism, economically, politically or culturally, and the ultimate outcome looked and functioned nothing like the 'original'.

Neoliberalism arrived as a much-awaited saviour (for capitalism) to bring some kind of order to this apparent mess, and in this sense it is the direct opposite of liberalism, whose primary function was to *subvert* the seemingly stable system secured by the feudal world (that is, European) order that was built on strict hierarchies in the family, land distribution, production and belief systems, a system where everybody 'knew their places'. The only thing that neoliberalism subverted, however, was the control mechanisms imposed on the market by the state, shattering the illusion that the state was the representative of the entire people against any external or internal threats to its well-being. In a very short time span, it managed to establish, in Foucault's words, a 'market economy without *laissez-faire*', a world-system in which any freedom that endangered the unrestrained freedom of the market was summarily supressed by the state. In this 'neo' version,

> Liberalism, far from being a doctrine that was antistate in essence, became the central justification for the strengthening of the efficacy of the state machinery. This was because liberals saw the state as essential to achieving their central objective furthering the modernity of technology while simultaneously judiciously appeasing the dangerous classes. They hoped thereby to check the precipitate implications of the concept of the sovereignty of the 'people' that were derived from a modernity of liberation. (Wallerstein 1995, 132)

This 'victory' of neoliberalism, however, was quite short-lived. Many a sign were already visible on the horizon, but in four decades, ending roughly with the 2008 crisis in the US (eventually inflicting the entire globe), it became quickly obsolete and started its meteoric descent, culminated in the global crisis of 2020, enhanced by an unexpected factor, the Covid-19 pandemic.

The Boy Who Cried 'Wolf!'

Marxists are often accused of crying 'Wolf!' constantly, predicting the 'ultimate crisis' of capitalism every twenty years or so, since 1848. It is hard to claim that there isn't a grain of truth in these accusations, and to tell the truth, some Marxists have indeed been a bit trigger-happy with their predictions of doom, or 'good tidings' of an end to capitalism many times. Even non-Marxists have gotten their share of this blame: Nouriel Roubini, an American Economist, who correctly predicted the 2008 crisis in the US years ahead, was first greeted with enthusiasm and made into a popular figure, even a celebrity-soothsayer, but when he continued his predictions and started to comment on the unsustainability of capitalism, he was quickly discarded and cancelled out from the mainstream media. Nowadays, he is only remembered and pejoratively referred to as 'Dr. Doom', if at all. This, indeed, seems to be the destiny of most truth-tellers, when the truth they tell does not coincide with what people wish to hear, rather than that of downright liars, because liars usually tell you exactly what you want to hear, instead of the truth. Gandalf in *The Lord of the Rings*, for instance, is one such truth-teller, and when he brings evil tidings (which he usually does), he is met with doubt and animosity: 'I greet you, [...] and maybe you look for welcome. But truth to tell your welcome is doubtful here, Master Gandalf. You have ever been a herald of woe. Troubles follow you like crows, and ever the oftener the worse. Why should I welcome you, Gandalf Stormcrow?'[6] When you run ahead of troubles to warn people of them, they automatically believe that troubles follow you, because for millennia, and in reality and fiction alike, '*post hoc, ergo propter hoc*' has been peremptorily accepted as a self-evident principle, no matter how many times philosophers, logicians and thinkers warn people against it.

Since I belong to this peculiar group of stormcrows who are accused of crying 'Wolf!' all the time, I would like to analyse that particular Aesop Tale that made the term 'Crying Wolf!' famous a little more closely.

In the tale by Aesop, a shepherd boy alerts the nearby villagers by crying 'Wolf!' every once in a while, and when they take up arms and rush to help, he snickers at them. One day the much-dreaded wolf really comes, but this time the villagers pay no heed to his cries, and the wolf eats all the sheep. The moral of the tale, according to Aesop, is, 'There is no believing a liar, even when he speaks the truth.' Is it so, really? Aesop, and following him, all those who refuse to believe in the cries of 'Wolf!', seem to forget one very important detail: the sheep eaten by the wolf do not belong to the boy, who is probably paid a meagre amount to watch the sheep, but to the villagers themselves. All right, you idiots, you have proved to us how clever you are by not believing 'the liar' and making fun of him—and lost all your sheep in the process! You may not be aware of it, but the joke is on you! You should either have fired the boy who took pleasure in deceiving you a long time ago, or you should at least have made sure that there is no wolf by double-checking. We should at least have learned from the Epimenides Paradox, almost as ancient as the Aesop Fable, that the

---

[6] J.R.R. Tolkien (2004), The Two Towers, in The Lord of The Rings: 50th Anniversary Edition, Harper Collins, 512-13.

opposite of 'All Cretans are liars!' is not 'All Cretans tell the truth all the time!', but only 'Not all Cretans lie all the time!' The shepherd boy may or may not be telling the truth, even though he is an established liar, so, go check! The moral of this tale should be rather, 'Don't be so cocksure of your own cleverness, when the ones who stand to lose the most is you.'

Slavoj Žižek asserted in the Introduction to his 2010 book, *Living in the End Times*, that:

> the global capitalist system is approaching an apocalyptic zero-point. Its 'four riders of the apocalypse' are comprised by the ecological crisis, the consequences of the biogenetic revolution, imbalances within the system itself (problems with intellectual property; forthcoming struggles over raw materials, food and water), and the explosive growth of social divisions and exclusions (Žižek 2010, x).

He does not, in his usual daredevilry, hesitate to use the word 'apocalypse', and lists the particular 'four horsemen' for this particular apocalypse as: (i) the ecological crisis which is quickly approaching catastrophic proportions; (ii) biogenetic technologies that radically change both production and the definition of 'humanity'; (iii) the inability of 'private property' to hold everything together as the bonding agent of capitalism; and (iv) the meteoric rise of inequalities and the desperate mobility thereof, both on local and global scales. Many have blamed him in the past for his use of language for an exaggerated 'shock-value' from time to time, sometimes justifiably, but are we going to do the same this time, especially after a decade that did nothing but confirm what he said? Is it possible that this boy had been telling the truth just this once?

We are surrounded by the howls of the wolves. They heralded their coming since the end of the last century: People don't feel loyal to the boundaries of the nation-state anymore, but immigrating, migrating, translocating (or trying to do so) constantly all around the world; not out of sheer fickleness, not to prove a point, but out of real, crucial, inescapable and sometimes fatal need. The 'precious' of the capitalist world-system, private property, cannot hold fast against the new production technologies developed by capitalism itself, against what we may call 'digital reproduction' that transgresses the walls of the factories and offices, as well as cities, nations and continents. People don't believe in the lies and half-truths daily manufactured by the media, by the political edifice, by the leaders and self-styled 'experts' anymore. Nor do they believe the fundamental scientific truths (transient and partial, maybe, but nevertheless truths) honoured for centuries, *and necessary*, if we are to be able to communicate with each other. They just don't know what to believe in anymore. Revered institutions of education have neglected educating the coming generations for a better life in their haste to become profitable and 'useful'—and ended up being neither. The disintegration of 'truth' is also dissolving millennia-old *moral* prerogatives in human relations, family values, sexuality and gender relations (not necessarily a bad thing in itself), but it is also corroding *ethical* values (a great calamity), throwing the baby out of the window along with the wash-water. Any moron with half a grain of so-called 'charisma', a bit of cunning, and a propensity for demagoguery (given the correct economic and political connections and network, of course) can become a populist leader now. We have already, albeit grudgingly, given up our arrogant claim of subjugating nature to our will, and are fighting a defensive and desperate war just to survive, fatally hampered by the equally defensive and desperate struggle of capitalism to weather this crisis unharmed and unchanged, an act of futility in itself.

It might be the season to take stormcrows seriously when so much is at stake; but of course, the choice is yours.

'What Next?'

Yevgeny Ivanovic Zamyatin wrote in 1923, in the midst of one of the most turbulent times of the past century, that:

> Today we can look and think only as men do in the face of death: we are about to die—and what did it all mean? How have we lived? If we could start all over, from the beginning, what would we live by? And for what? What we need in literature today are vast philosophic horizons seen from mastheads, from airplanes; we need the most ultimate, the most fearsome, the most fearless 'Why?' and 'What next?' (Zamyatin 1923 [1970], 109-10)

He said this only six years after the Russian Revolution, with the Bolshevik Party slowly but decidedly turning into Stalin's playground; five years after the end of the First World War (or the first chapter of the Thirty Years War of the 20th Century, whichever way you want to see it); five years after the defeat of the German Revolution by the Social Democrats themselves; only one year after Mussolini became the Prime Minister in Italy; and the same year as Hitler's notorious Beer-Hall-Putsch of Munich. Two years before, in 1921, Zamyatin's *We*, arguably the first modern dystopian novel, had become the first book banned by the Soviet Board of Censors. Eight years later, in 1931, he appealed to Stalin himself to be let go into voluntary exile, since he was not allowed to publish anything in the USSR, and went to France, to die there in 1937 as a broken man, not able to write anymore.

Almost a century after he wrote those words, we seem to be facing a similar ordeal: The coming few decades will also be extremely tumultuous and most probably decisive in the future of a multitude of things: not only of specific nation-states; not only of (neo)liberalism or capitalism as a whole; not only even of humanity, but also of the entire planet. Already, there are, here and there, some transient 'victories' or 'defeats' depending on which point of view you take, none of them in themselves conclusive. Donald J. Trump, for instance, who appeared to be the token representative of ascendant proto-fascist populism, is defeated in the November 2020 US Elections, and is discharged from the White House (we will yet to see whether it will be 'dishonourably' enough or not), despite all the conspiracy theories he keeps conjuring up and the considerable paramilitary racist forces he seems to command. But still, we should pay heed to Bertolt Brecht's warning in the closing lines of *The Resistible Rise of Arturo Ui,* a satiric parody of Hitler's rise to power, which are added as a postscript to the play he completed in 1941,[7] years before the conclusive defeat of Adolf Hitler:

> Therefore learn how to see and not to gape.
> To act instead of talking all day long.
> The world was almost won by such an ape!
> The nations put him where his kind belong.
> But don't rejoice too soon at your escape -
> The womb he crawled from is still going strong.

Those of us who eagerly await an automatic and spontaneous purge of capitalism after the disintegration of (neo)liberalism, and the arrival of a more egalitarian and libertarian (or, to use Balibar's neologism, 'equalibertarian') world-order, should stop holding our breaths, because such a thing will almost definitely not happen. As a matter of fact, nothing significant can ever come to pass without those who expect a different/better world endeavouring actively to make it happen. To put it more precisely, what will happen after the existing order crumbles, is *exactly what we do during the course of its downfall*: it is not preordained one way or another. [8] It is the sum total of how we organise, what goals we set for ourselves, how we militate against it, how we envision the future, how we communicate different (and sometimes conflicting) 'utopias' to each other, what we learn from the existing practical struggles against it, how we try to participate in, try to influence, but more importantly, *how we are guided by* such struggles. Wallerstein had called this composite and joint effort a

---

[7] Although it was completed in 1941, the play was not produced in the US, where Brecht was living in exile at the time. It was only produced in 1958, almost two decades after it was written and after Brecht's death; the above stanza was added later (no, Brecht was not clairvoyant!) In 1941 the US was still at peace with Nazi Germany, waiting on the sidelines for a 'profitable' outcome from the clash between major European Powers, *until* it was willy-nilly drawn into the fray in 1942. Unfortunately, a Pearl Harbour always seems to be necessary to shake and nudge US politicians and public sentiment into anti-fascist action. Let us hope that the attempt at 'Storming the Capitol' by the Trumpist mob on January 6, 2021 will serve as a modern-day Pearl Harbour.

[8] We should not, of course, interpret this as 'anything is possible'. It is not preordained, but within given parameters:

> Men make their own history, but they do not make it as they please; they do not make it under self-selected circumstances, but under circumstances existing already, given and transmitted from the past. The tradition of all dead generations weighs like a nightmare on the brains of the living. And just as they seem to be occupied with revolutionizing themselves and things, creating something that did not exist before, precisely in such epochs of revolutionary crisis they anxiously conjure up the spirits of the past to their service, borrowing from them names, battle slogans, and costumes in order to present this new scene in world history in time-honored disguise and borrowed language. (Marx 2010, 103-4)

'multilogue':

> We must engage in an enormous worldwide multilogue, for the solutions are by no means evident. And those who wish to continue the present under other guises are very powerful. The end of what modernity? Let it be the end of false modernity, and the onset, for the first time, of a true modernity of liberation (Wallerstein 1995, 144).

'An enormous worldwide multilogue', especially back in 1995, seems to be an extremely ambitious project when looking back on the quarter century since then, during which time, despite all the significant (even historical) events taking place, little was done to coordinate a global agora to share alternative prospects of the future, let alone a (or several) worldwide initiative(s). Meanwhile, a 'multilogue' of capitalist nation-states and multinational corporations was still in effect, although the peculiarities and unruliness of the new-fangled 'populist' leaders appeared to be hindering such cooperation. Most of us were scandalised, for instance, by Trump's cavalier disengagement from international accords and organisations, but he nevertheless kept strong (albeit unreliable) ties with his 'peers': he was BFFs with Russian autocrat Putin, made 'good friends' with North Korean tyrant Kim Jong Un, and was always on good terms with Turkish strongman Erdoğan, in spite of some publicised quarrels (if his former National Security Adviser John Bolton is to be believed[9]). He heartily applauded Brasilian populist/autocrat Bolsonaro's election and was always a good ally despite all his grotesque antics. Notwithstanding his almost automatic response of blaming 'Djina' for almost everything going wrong in the world, and the irrational trade war he initiated with China, he was the first to rush in to applaud President Xi when he changed the Chinese Constitution to remain President for life.[10]

It was not much different in the rest of the world: Turkish President Erdoğan who proudly claims to be the protector of the Moslems everywhere in the world, has no qualms to be close buddies with India's Modi, who carries out a covert almost-genocide against the Moslem population in India. In the same vein, he became something of a hero among Arab/Moslem peoples and especially the Palestinians when he defied Israeli President Shimon Peres in

---

[9] See Bolton 2020, *passim*. Bolton claims to be present in the Oval Office during many phone conversations between Trump and Erdoğan throughout 2018-19, and underlines the 'buddy' tone in most of them.

[10] The poster-boy of US proto-fascist populism, Steve Bannon, who was the mastermind behind the Trump Campaign in 2016, and later Trump's 'Chief Strategist' until August 2017, is a very good example of the international coordination efforts of contemporary populism. He is quoted to say, 'All I'm trying to be is the infrastructure, globally, for the global populist movement.' (Horowitz 2018) Since he was fired from his relatively comfortable position in the White House, he made a grand tour of populist groups and organisations in Europe for this purpose, among them Orban's *Fidesz* (Hungary), the Five Star Movement (Italy), the *AfD* (Germany), the *Rassemblement national* (France), the *PiS* (Poland), the *SD* (Sweden), Wilders' *PVV* (Netherlands), the *FPÖ* (Austria), the UK Independence Party, *Vox* (Spain), the UK Conservative Party, Dodik's *SNSD* (Serbia), and *Likud* (Israel—not in Europe, but close enough).

Davos in 2009, but sees no harm in keeping very close economic and political ties with Netanyahu, who is a much worse antagonist than Peres for the Palestinians, and a proven embezzler to boot. When the Chinese Government embarks upon a covert almost-genocide against the Uighur population in China, both Muslims, and Turks (at least very close relatives), the 'protector' is again tongue-tied, because China is a prospective alternative-ally in the international power-play he is engaged in.

Similar stories can be told about the new-fangled populist leaders around the world: Brasil's Jair Bolsonaro; Hungary's Victor Orban; Russia's Vladimir Putin; China's Xi Jinping; North Korea's Kim Jong Un; Israel's Benjamin Netanyahu; UK's Boris Johnson; the list seems to grow with each passing day. Although most of these leaders are flagrant narcissists, self-centred and unruly to the point of grotesqueness, and although they seem to pay no heed to established diplomatic conventions, they still find ways to retain a certain equilibrium among themselves which keeps the neoliberal/capitalist world-order going, albeit stumblingly and in fits and starts.

Unfortunately, the same thing cannot be said about the newly emerging anti-systemic movements. Although they do exist since the commencement of the anti- (and later, alter-) globalisation movements, roughly starting in Seattle in 1999 and continuing until today, reaching peaks in Occupy Wall Street (in the US and partially the UK) in 2011, in the Arab Spring throughout 2010-2012, in the Gezi Commune in Turkey in 2013, most of them either dwindled down, or were hijacked (as it happened in the Arab Spring, by radical jihadists), and did not leave durable organisational residues behind. The 2017 Women's March against Trump in the US quickly expanded to gain a transnational character, and lent momentum to the Abortion Law victories in Ireland (2018) and Argentina (2020), and the massive movement against the Abortion Ban in Poland, although it was partially defeated in 2020. The Hong Kong demonstrations of 2019-2020 against the authoritarian legal system imposed by China were next. The last one in this string of events is the Black Lives Matter movement in the US, starting symbolically with Colin Kaepernick's 'knee' in 2016, and becoming a considerable mass movement in 2020. It is, however, still too early to comment on the prospective transnational impact of these last three events. Among the more extensive organisational steps, mostly from within the establishment, we can enumerate the progressive thrust in the US by Bernie Sanders (2016-2020) which was pushed back by the joint efforts of the conservative elements within the Democratic Party, and the equally strong thrust by Jeremy Corbyn in the UK (2015-19), which was likewise pushed back, due to both the conservative reaction from within the Labour Party (using accusations of 'anti-Semitism' as a conservative weapon), and the defeat in the 2019 elections, which ended up in the rapid (but hopefully short-lived) rise of Boris Johnson, yet another grotesque populist leader.

So, what next?

Although few of the above movements would call themselves 'communist' as such, the below description of 'The Communists' by Marx and Engels during the 1848 revolutions still apply, *mutatis mutandis*:

> The Communists do not form a separate party opposed to other working-class parties.
>
> They have no interests separate and apart from those of the proletariat as a whole.
>
> They do not set up any sectarian ['separate' in the first edition—BS] principles of their own, by which to shape and mould the proletarian movement.
>
> The Communists are distinguished from the other working-class parties by this only: 1. In the national struggles of the proletarians of the different countries, they point out and bring to the front the common interests of the entire proletariat, independently of all nationality. 2. In the various stages of development which the struggle of the working class against the bourgeoisie has to pass through, they always and everywhere represent the interests of the movement as a whole. (Marx & Engels 2010, 497)

Marx and Engels insist that the communists are *only one of the parties* of the working class, *with no sectarian or separate interests or principles of their own*. They do not try to 'shape and mould' the movement; they differ from other parties in two issues only: they act as a *transnational reminder* of the overall agenda of the struggle in local/national movements; and they act as the *historical prompter* of the struggle, as an embodiment of a memory, so to speak, that consistently reminds what had happened before, and what results were achieved or failed to come to pass. Every living and growing movement active today desperately needs such reminders, in order not to repeat the mistakes of the past, and not to find temporary solutions to local/national/identity problems at the cost of other localities, other parts of the world and other identities.

So, you don't even need to be a communist, or specifically speak about the working class, because, as you can follow throughout the above paragraph, I have disappeared both terms with a sleight of hand, and what Marx and Engels were suggesting did not lose an iota of significance: all organised structures within movements vying for liberation, equality and a better life can follow this agenda in their struggles against a disintegrating neoliberal capitalism, and, more importantly, an authoritarian and/or totalitarian dictatorship, eagerly waiting in the wings for its turn to come.

What Next (in this Book)?

Wallerstein had suggested that,

Our task today, and for the next fifty years is the task of utopistics. It is the task of imagining, and struggling to create this new social order. For it is by no means assured that the end of one inegalitarian historical system will result in a better one. The struggle is quite open. We need today to define the concrete institutions through which human liberation can finally be expressed. We have lived through its pretended expression in our existing world-system, in which liberal ideology tried to persuade us of a reality that the liberals were in fact struggling against—the reality of increasing equality and democracy. And we have lived through the disillusionment of failed antisystemic movements, movements that were themselves part of the problem as much as they were a part of the solution. (Wallerstein 1995, 144)

If we are to accept his counsel, it becomes clear that a book, a collection of essays by a single person, or a more extensive collection of essays and articles by multiple authors will not be enough even to scratch the surface of this colossal task. Any attempt to 'define the concrete institutions through which human liberation can finally be expressed,' should necessarily be a part of a greater effort consisting of books, articles, essays and countless other ways of communicating with each other, imagining networks both on local and global levels. It should cover a span of at least several decades, dissecting and critiquing both the failing present world-system, and its alleged alternatives developed throughout the last two centuries. It should be a 'utopia which is not a utopia', not something springing from a writer's (or a host of writers') minds, imagination and good wishes, like Athena from Zeus' head, but from a lively and open-ended utopian discussion rooted in the 'existing class struggle, from a historical movement going on under our very eyes.' (Marx & Engels 1848 [2010])

In this book, I tried to (begin to) do my part, by sharing some ideas on *some* of the issues at hand. I did not touch on many important matters like the huge environmental crisis which will eventually take up an ever-increasing part of our agenda in the very near future, since I lack the necessary scientific background on the crisis itself. Likewise, I did not try to comment on the imminent advent of (and projected crises arising from) Artificial Intelligence and the discussions about Post-Humanity accompanying it, because, again, these areas need more focused and targeted scientific research. I only briefly commented on the causes and outcomes of the rapidly growing immigration crisis throughout the globe, and tried to put forward some arguments (again briefly) on 'identity politics' as opposed to class-politics (see 'The Psychopolitics of the Entitled Victim' below).

What I *did* (or tried to) do is as follows:

In 'On Radical Ambiguity', I try to make a rather theoretical introduction for the following, more concrete, arguments, by problematising the concepts of 'Knowledge' and 'Truth', taking Simone de Beauvoir's *Pour une morale de l'ambiguité* as a guiding light, challenging both Fundamentalist and 'Enlightenment' absolutisms, and proceed to propose an 'Ambiguous' approach to Truth which is nevertheless radical, critical and linked to revolutionary praxis.

In 'The Midas Blessing', I argue that the new (digital) technologies under neoliberalism necessarily come into irresolvable conflict with the existing relations of production, or the regime of private property. To keep free-sharing under strict control, the sectors dependent on 'intellectual property', in complicity with existing governments, resort to authoritarian (and increasingly totalitarian) measures. As a result, many intellectuals, writers, composers and producers face a serious ethical dilemma: Whether 'tis nobler in the mind to become accomplices with the authoritarian, 1984-like strategies of these sectors, or to give their creations/productions away as *gifts*, from which the overwhelming majority of them do not earn a living anyway.

In 'The End of Truth as We Know It', I suggest that the disappearance of Truth started with the 'Neoliberal Takeover of Higher Education', which resulted in the *ultimate dissociation of information from knowledge*, by making universities purveyors of practical and 'useful' (that is, useful for the capitalist establishment) information and gradually dismantling 'useless' knowledge production in the form of humanities, liberal arts and social sciences. The re-enfranchisement of University Discourse can only be done through a meaningful effort by scholars and intellectuals from 'both sides of the fence', the victims of both the so-called 'democratic' neoliberal establishments and the violent attacks by the contemporary right-wing populist establishments in so-called 'modernising' countries.

In '*The Game of Thrones* as a Failed Attempt at Universal Populism', I try to problematise the attempts to 'read' the last season of the TV show, *The Game of Thrones,* as an 'in-depth' and extensive commentary on contemporary politics, complete with observations on populism, comparative government, democracy, feminism, multiculturalism, etc. Many, including some prominent thinkers and political figures, have taken the side of Queen Daenerys Targaryen, imagining her as a representative of 'the people', and her (failed) bid for absolute power as an attempt to create a more libertarian society. I argue that rather than being taken in by the effort to combine the object of desire and the Big Other in Daenerys' personality, we should (re)start thinking and acting in terms of different and fundamentally conflicted entities presumably within 'the people', genders, races, sexual (and also various other) orientations, and, of course, classes.

Finally, in 'The Psychopolitics of the Entitled Victim' I argue that Populism is the coincidence and intersection of the ideologies and movements built on the (exceedingly suspect) axiom that 'the People' is an actually existing agency in and of itself, as one of the poles of the dimorphism, 'the people/the elite'. No universalised concept, however, can be created in a vacuum; so, Populism has to invent an (horizontal) adversary, an antagonist against which the populists can declare themselves protagonists. This adversary can be other nations, a neighbouring country or 'imperialism' in general, and their 'internal collaborators'. Populists also need a social stratum *lower than 'the people' itself*, another (vertical) adversary, another *subject* that is supposed to be *subjected to* its will, that is, the immigrants, refugees, the *Ausländer*, the 'aliens'. No populism can exist without creating or 'inventing' these third elements, and this is precisely the reason why all claims to a 'left' populism are destined to turn, eventually, into their opposite, right-wing populism, which is quickly turning into a massive authoritarian/autocratic global wave, reminiscent of, but not exactly identical with Fascism/Nazism.

CHAPTER 1

ON RADICAL AMBIGUITY

... Between the deliberate falsehood and the disinterested inaccuracy it is very hard to distinguish sometimes... To deceive deliberately – that is one thing. But to be so sure of your facts, of your ideas and their essential truth that the details do not matter – that, my friend is a special characteristic of particularly honest persons... She looks down and sees Jane Wilkinson in the hall. No doubt enters her head that it *is* Jane Wilkinson. She knows it is. She says she saw her face distinctly because – being so sure of her facts – exact details do not matter! It is pointed out to her that she could not have seen her face. Is that so? Well, what does it matter if she saw her face or not – it *was* Jane Wilkinson... She *knows*. And so she answers questions in the light of her knowledge, not by reason of remembered facts. The positive witness should always be treated with suspicion, my friend. The uncertain witness who doesn't remember, isn't sure, will think a minute – ah! yes, that's how it was – is infinitely more to be depended upon!
Hercule Poirot in *Lord Edgware Dies* by Agatha Christie, 1933.

$\Delta x \, \Delta p \geq \frac{\hbar}{2}$: The more precisely the position is determined, the less precisely the momentum is known in this instant, and vice versa.
Werner Heisenberg, *Uncertainty Paper*, 1927.

In 1933, Hercule Poirot, the fictional sleuth of Agatha Christie who solves every puzzle using his 'little grey cells', demonstrates the futility of 'positive knowledge', how it goads its (supposed) possessor into ignoring the details, and since facts not yet framed in a semantic context always assume the character of details, into ignoring the facts, hence bending, distorting, recreating and misrepresenting them in order to conform to a pre-existing, *a priori* 'knowledge'. Werner Heisenberg, however, precisely six years before Poirot, demonstrates the *impossibility* of such knowledge, basing his argument (as a proper scientist always should) not on the undesirable consequences of presumed positive knowledge, but rather on its premises: 'But what is wrong in the sharp formulation of the law of causality, "When we know the present precisely, we can predict the future," is not the conclusion but the assumption. Even in principle we cannot know the present in all detail.' (Heisenberg 1983) What Heisenberg suggests actually coincides with Poirot's argument: The further we go into detail in our investigation of physical phenomena, the less precise we get. The problem arises when we do not acknowledge this fact and believe our knowledge (of larger, more general physical phenomena) to be absolute, applicable to everything in existence, from the movement of galaxies to the movement of photons and electrons. Therefore, the more we believe our presumed knowledge to be *certain*, the more likely we are to ignore the minute details (the momentum and/or the position of an electron, for instance) which do not conform to this knowledge. To be sure, the 1926 discussion between Heisenberg and Einstein makes a specification as to the nature of this 'knowledge': While Heisenberg tries to specify observable/knowable phenomena with regard to measurability, Einstein challenges him to suggest that observability is directly connected with conformity to a certain theory:

> Heisenberg: 'One cannot observe the electron orbits inside the atom. [...]but since it is reasonable to consider only those quantities in a theory that can be measured, it seemed natural to me to introduce them only as entities, as representatives of electron orbits, so to speak.'

> Einstein: 'But you don't seriously believe that only observable quantities should be considered in a physical theory?'

> 'I thought this was the very idea that your Relativity Theory is based on?' Heisenberg asked in surprise.

> 'Perhaps I used this kind of reasoning,' replied Einstein, 'but it is nonsense nevertheless. [...] In reality the opposite is true: only the theory decides what can be observed.' (Heisenberg 1969)

Isn't this exactly what Poirot was criticizing? To bend observable facts in order for them to conform to a pre-conceived knowledge, of a certainty? It seems to be so, unless we take into account a (seemingly) slight shift in terminology: While Poirot is talking about *knowledge* (even *positive* knowledge), Einstein is referring to *theory*, that is, *theoria*, that is, a *gaze*, an outlook, an *Anschauung*. Theory, in the most basic sense of the term, is the way you look at things, and therefore, it goes without saying that it 'decides what can be observed.'

Knowledge, on the other hand, is something *arrived at*, and once you arrive there, there is no room for uncertainties: So, if details (facts) tend to create unwanted uncertainties, it goes without saying that you should ignore or distort them. Theory is based on uncertainties; the gaze shifts, wanders, wonders, takes in new data, changes, mutates: it represents the uneasy equilibrium of *a priori* and *a posteriori*. *Positive* knowledge, on the other hand, once established, becomes fixed; it doesn't look anymore, it tells facts what they ought to be: it represents the hegemony of *a priori* over *a posteriori*. In short, once the theoretical act coagulates into knowledge, which will become, in the blink of an eye, *preconceived knowledge*, and loses its self-reflexivity, it becomes a peril, rather than an asset, for further knowledge.

In this sense, positive knowledge, that is, knowledge unquestionably certain of itself, has the possibility of becoming the bedrock of what we today call Fundamentalism, once the *gaze* is fixed. But wait, Poirot's uncertain witness will say, isn't the same positive knowledge also the basis of the Enlightenment, what we know today as the diametrical opposite of Fundamentalism? Nonsense, the positive witness will answer, the same thing cannot be the basis of two diametrically opposite entities, can it now? The uncertain witness remains ambiguous and demands (or requests, depending on their predilection) a further examination of the concepts of 'Fundamentalism' and 'Enlightenment', with which I will try to comply.

Fundamentalist Knowledge

Let us consider the poles of the Fundamentalism versus Enlightenment duality more closely: Fundamentalism is a term much used and abused these days, and it is usually coupled with Islam and terrorism (by conservative-liberals), and religious bigotry in general (by liberals in general). The former, narrower meaning is a specific tactical use by neo-conservatives in the rationalization of their global power-politics, so I will deal with it later. In the broader liberal terminology, Fundamentalism means everything that the Enlightenment was against. It is supposed to stand against critical thought and reason, since some fundamental truths are axiomatic for it. Fundamentalists (of Islamic, Christian and Judaist creed) start from presumptions that are not questionable, not open to critical inquiry or to change over time.

The main problem with fundamentalism seems to be that, fundamentalists always positively *know* that they are right. Once, for instance, you accept as a fact that the *Koran* is God's Holy Word, there will be no mention of questioning the political, economic or cultural structure of the society in which you live (as long as it is established according to the principles outlined in the Holy Book), because everything is clearly stated there, from gender relations to inheritance laws, from public administration to the rules that should be followed while buying and selling camels. Conversely, if the society in which you live is not organised according to the book, then you have the right to use every means to transform it. The same thing applies in the other religious structures too: Once you accept the Bible as God's Truth, you *know* that the universe was created in only six days, that women should be subservient to men, because, first, they were created as a second thought, just to keep company, and, second, they were the instruments of the original sin. Judaist Fundamentalism seems to be the most tightly organised of them all, since it also entails a racial prejudice along with the religious one, and does not make any allowances even for assimilation. Judaist fundamentalists simply *know* that the Jews are God's chosen.

This positive knowledge which stands outside, even opposed to, reason, gives the fundamentalists the superior ethical position to patronise, silence, suppress, oppress and finally annihilate any and all opposing or even sceptical views and positions, since they positively *know* that the opposition is wrong. This ethical position is the basis for *Jihad* and the Crusades as extroverted or extrapunitive fundamentalist acts ('Since we know we are right, everybody should be *made* to share this knowledge'); or for the self-imposed Jewish closing-in, which is introverted and intropunitive ('We are right, but *they* will never know'). Since the basis of all knowledge is a set of unquestionable statements embedded (even hidden, as they are in the case of the *Kabbalah*) in some holy texts, there is the necessity for a privileged group of people who know and interpret these texts, and guide the rest along the lines drawn in them. This position of guidance is precisely what Kant, as the philosopher *par excellence* of the Enlightenment, criticised in his definitive essay, *What is the Enlightenment*. When the rest (or some of them) refuse to be guided, there is only one course of action open to fundamentalist guides: Coerce them, and when it fails, punish them. This is the reason why, although 'Thou shalt not kill!' is one of the primary commandments of all monotheistic religions, they never fail to enforce the capital punishment, most of the time arbitrarily.

The *Auto-da-Fé* constitutes some kind of a zenith among the ultimate acts of fundamentalism, and the curious thing about it was, in spite of the horrors committed, it was not born out of pure malice, but rather made a claim (albeit a false one) to compassion: The shepherd, Cardinal Tomás de Torquemada was leading the herd away from the ultimate danger of damnation by torturing their bodies in order to save their souls. In Dostoyevsky's *Brothers Karamazov*, Ivan tells Alyosha of a story of Torquemada condemning Jesus to death again, this time in 15th century Seville. The old, wizened Grand Inquisitor comes to (still young) Jesus' cell at night and reproaches him for what he's done:

> Was it not you who so often said then: "I want to make you free"? But now you have seen these "free" men, [...] Yes, this work has cost us dearly, [...] but we have finally finished this work in your name. For fifteen hundred years we have been at pains over this freedom, but now it is finished, and well finished. You do not believe that it is well finished? [...] Know, then, that now, precisely now, these people are more certain than ever before that they are completely free, and at the same time they themselves have brought us their freedom and laid it at our feet. It is our doing, but is it what you wanted? This sort of freedom? [...] For only now [...] has it become possible to think for the first time about human happiness. Man was made a rebel; can rebels be happy? [... Y]ou rejected the only way of arranging for human happiness, but fortunately, on your departure, you handed the work over to us. You promised, you established with your word, you gave us the right to bind and loose, and surely you cannot even think of taking this right away from us now. Why, then, have you come to interfere with us? (Dostoevsky 1992, 212-213)

Jesus (if he ever existed) was not a Fundamentalist as a person; he was ambiguous to the last moment on the cross, always questioning. That was the gist of his teaching to people: 'I will make you free.' Free to doubt, free to be ambivalent, never to be self-assured even when you are going to die for what you (probably) believe to be true. Torquemada, on the other hand, *knew* that this freedom was too much for the people, his herd. The burden of doubt, of ambiguity, of choice must be taken from the people in order to make them happy. Torquemada is the true Fundamentalist in this equation, just like Moses was. When Moses and his God tried to coerce the Pharaoh to 'let Israelites go', most of what they did would have seemed terrorist acts by today's standards:

> [...] And the LORD spake unto Moses, Say unto Aaron, Take thy rod, and stretch out thine hand upon the waters of Egypt, upon their streams, upon their rivers, and upon their ponds, and upon all their pools of water, that they may become blood; and that there may be blood throughout all the land of Egypt, both in vessels of wood, and in vessels of stone.

> [...] And if thou refuse to let them go, behold, I will smite all thy borders with frogs.

> [...] And the LORD did that thing on the morrow, and all the cattle of Egypt died: but of the cattle of the children of Israel died not one.

> [...] Else, if thou refuse to let my people go, behold, tomorrow will I bring the locusts into thy coast.

> [...] And Moses said, Thus saith the LORD, About midnight will I go out into the midst of Egypt: And all the firstborn in the land of Egypt shall die, from the first born of Pharaoh that sitteth upon his throne, even unto the firstborn of the maidservant that is behind the mill; and all the firstborn of beasts. (*Exodus, 7-1*)

These five acts, turning the water into blood (chemical warfare), causing a plague of frogs and then of locusts (biological warfare), killing the cattle (sabotaging production), and finally killing all the firstborns, most of whom should be innocent civilians, all sanctioned (indeed implemented) by a mean and unforgiving God, are what today's fundamentalist 'terrorists' are doing, or at least trying to do. It is possible, therefore, to say that after three and a half millennia, the main strategies of the fundamentalists have not at all changed. Once you believe you *know*, you can steal, sabotage, maim and kill indiscriminately, since it is for the greater good. And the greater good is... whatever you say it is, because you *know*. The problem with Fundamentalism is not only that it believes that there is an ultimate Truth behind all existence; it is also that it believes this Truth to be knowable in its entirety, and that a person, or some persons, already have access to such knowledge.

How Enlightened is the Enlightenment?

The Enlightenment is supposed to be humankind's rebellion against their guides who are supposed to *know*.[1] In Kant's words:

> *Enlightenment is the human being's emancipation from its self incurred immaturity. Immaturity* is the inability to make use of one's intellect without the direction of another. This immaturity is self-incurred when its cause does not lie in a lack of intellect, but rather in a lack of resolve and courage to make use of one's intellect without the direction of another. '*Sapere aude*! Have the courage to make use of your own intellect!' is hence the motto of enlightenment. (Kant 2006, 17)

Further along the essay, Kant makes it clear that he was not living in an 'enlightened' age, but 'in an age of Enlightenment', that is, Enlightenment is only an ideal rather than an achieved or to-be-achieved state, embodied in an ongoing process. Towards the end of his essay, he also warns his age not to try to set up laws and rules which are exempt from change:

> One generation cannot form an alliance and conspire to put a subsequent generation in such a position in which it would be impossible for the latter to expand its knowledge (particularly where such knowledge is so vital), to rid this knowledge of errors, and, more generally, to proceed along the path of enlightenment. That would be a violation of human nature, the original vocation of which consists precisely in this progress; and the descendants are thus perfectly entitled to reject those resolutions as having been made in an unjust and criminal way. (Kant, 20)

This warning, aside from reiterating the earlier statement that enlightenment was an ongoing process, also questions the claim that human knowledge is capable of attaining (or having attained) an eternal, unchangeable truth. So, if we are to judge the Enlightenment by Kant's conception of it, there seems to be no, or little residual fundamentalism in it: Enlightenment is described in Kant as a perpetual questioning of yesterday's axiomatic truths, although he cautions us this questioning should be in such a way in order not to upset the existing social structure, especially in areas in which organization, coordination and immediacy is vital, such as the military, where you have to 'obey first and/but argue later'.

Enlightenment, however, was not only Immanuel Kant, nor was it a solely philosophical enterprise. It was also the age in which a new ruling class who,

---

[1] I am well aware that my Enlightenment 'subject who is supposed to know' (*le sujet supposé savoir*) completely overlaps with Lacan's definition of the analyst. This is no mere coincidence: The main difference is that, in Lacan the subject who is 'supposed to know', the analyst, is completely aware of the fact that they *do not know*, and in fact the process of psychoanalysis is the gradual uncovering of this fact by the analysand. The problem with the Enlightenment subject is that they really believe that they know; the supposition is treated as fact. More on this later.

having (almost) acquired economic supremacy in the past century, was trying to reinforce this supremacy with political and ideological power. Although we cannot take a shortcut and say that Enlightenment was an exclusively bourgeois ideological enterprise, without a doubt it coincided with the bourgeoisie's ascent to political and ideological power, and in this sense its nature is quite ambiguous: on the one hand it bears the marks of independent scientific and intellectual minds, trying to pave the way for unhindered freedom of thought and self-development for all humankind; but on the other, its call for freedom is limited in practice to the bourgeoisie's need for it, namely, the need for a free *market*, the need for freedom from all pre-capitalist ties that hinder individuals from interacting in this market (that is, freely selling their labour-power and buying commodities), and, last but not least, the freedom of the working-class from the means of production. This is why many eminent Enlightenment thinkers sometimes seem inconsistent and even hypocritical: Voltaire, while arguing against slavery as such, still benefited from slave trade in a roundabout way, and was even 'delighted' when a slave trader offered to name his slave ship after him.[2] Of course Voltaire was not simply being hypocritical: he was only caught up in the inescapable ambiguity that was inherent in the Enlightenment.

The political/ethical face of the Enlightenment is less ambiguous: The American Declaration of Independence (some eighteen years before Kant's essay) was not free of 'fundamental' truths:

> We hold these truths to be self-evident, that all men are created equal, that they are endowed by their Creator with certain unalienable Rights, that among these are Life, Liberty and the pursuit of Happiness. (*Declaration of Independence*)

As a matter of fact, the phrase 'all men' only applied to white men, and furthermore it was precisely what it said: all *men*, and not women. To be sure, the Declaration was a giant step away from all men being subjects of the king, a step to be repeated and indeed enhanced in the French Revolution a decade later. But it is a sign that most Enlightenment political/ethical positions to come will share with what we call Fundamentalism the same self-assurance that they are in the right. This is what gave the Jacobins (definitely the legitimate

---

[2] And, by the way, the Enlightenment was precisely the age in which our present concept of 'Race' was developed, preparing the ground for 19th and 20th century racism (See the 8-volume *Concepts of Race in the Eighteenth Century* edited by Robert Bernasconi). Racist bigotry is usually fiercer than the religious one, and crimes committed in the name of 'race' (genocides) usually have a greater death-toll and more far-reaching consequences than those committed in the name of 'religion', at least in the last two centuries. Still, however, we do not categorise racism under fundamentalism, because it has its roots in Enlightenment ideology, in a kind of Enlightenment science (or rather pseudo-science), of first Lamarckian, and later social-Darwinist brands, in which the hierarchy of races is constructed 'scientifically'. So, it was no coincidence that the deportation/massacre of Armenians in the Ottoman Empire between 1915-18 was carried out by *Ittihat ve Terakki,* a political organization then in power with an agenda of Ottoman modernization and a watered-down ideology of pseudo-Enlightenment, rather than the older establishment which was definitely as fundamentalist and conservative, but at the same time more cosmopolitan and presumably less racist.

children of the Enlightenment) the right to annihilate all opposing political positions, and while they were at it, each other in the end. This is why all the children of the Enlightenment, from the most docile liberals to the Marxists, are ambiguous towards the French Revolution: both liberals and communists compete in declaring it *their* revolution, but at the same time they stumble over each other to disown the period from 1792 to 1796, because it is precisely this period that betrays the secret of what we may call 'Enlightenment politics'. When it is the ideology of an opposition, it stands for the questioning of all existing fundamentalist axioms that pass for truths. Once in power, however, it hastily starts to proclaim its own truths and defends them using the same methods it has learned from its Fundamentalist ancestors.

In his famous *Leben des Galilei*, Bertolt Brecht creates a scene in which the basic idea of the Enlightenment (that of the scientist, represented by Galileo's pupil Andrea Sarti) is confronted with that of Fundamentalism (represented by the Catholic Inquisition). Sarti, his mother (Galileo's housekeeper) and Galileo's daughter have been waiting outside the chambers of the Inquisition where Galileo was being tried. When the bells begin to toll, signalling that Galileo has repented, his pupil Sarti, who had been hoping for his master to hold fast, to denounce the Inquisition, begins to yell: 'And the sun is the centre of the cosmos and motionless, and the earth is not the centre and not motionless.'[3] Of course we don't know that this actually happened, as a historical fact; it is as speculative as the great master mumbling '*Eppur si muove,*' while leaving the chambers (which statement, by the way, Brecht does not use). What Brecht seems to be trying to do, however, is to show us that Fundamentalism and 'Enlightenment' use the same basic syntax. We, as citizens of a more enlightened age, *know* for a fact that the sun, indeed, does *not* stand still, and far from being the centre of the universe, it is a very ordinary star at the outskirts of one galaxy among many. The scientist, making some of the necessary observations, may be pretty sure that the existing dominant ideological preconceptions (those of the Ptolemaic universe in this case) are definitely false. But once they try to replace these preconceptions with newer, affirmative ones, they start using the same syntax. The problem with Sarti is, as the precursor and, in Brecht's play indeed the archetype, of the Enlightenment scientist-cum-ideologist, he is as sure of himself as the Inquisitors inside the chambers. The only thing he lacks is power, and that, the Sartis of the coming centuries will have in abundance.

We could start to see that our basic dichotomy, that of Enlightenment versus Fundamentalism, is a little bit more complicated than what it first seemed: Fundamentalism syntactically includes Enlightenment ideology, and

---

[3] Andrea Sarti: *Und die Sonne ist das Zentrum der Welt und unbeweglich an ihrem Ort, und die Erde ist nicht Zentrum und nicht unbeweglich.* (Brecht 1963, 127)

Enlightenment, in its adherence to some fundamental (or 'self-evident') truths, axioms which seem to be neutral and objective, but prove to be socially conditioned on close inspection, albeit they are different from those of *religious* Fundamentalism, is essentially fundamentalist. What we perceive as *radicalism* in the political and ideological attitude of the Enlightenment and Enlightenment-inspired belief systems, then, is not radicalism at all, but just another aspect of fundamentalism. Radicalism is 'grasping things by the root'; Enlightenment-inspired ideologies, however, do not grasp things by the root, but rather leave the 'root' (of absolute faith in a set of axioms) intact, while aggressively striving to substitute religious axioms with another set of their own. Our dichotomy then metamorphoses into another one between two fundamentalisms, one religious and the other 'scientific' (rationalistic or positivistic).

About a century and a half ago, in a text they never published, and in a footnote probably written for their eyes only, for purposes of self-clarification –since they never repeated it in their later work– Marx and Engels said:

> We know only a single science, the science of history. One can look at history from two sides and divide it into the history of nature and the history of men. The two sides are. however, inseparable: the history of nature and the history of men are dependent on each other so long as men exist. The history of nature, called natural science, does not concern us here; but we will have to examine the history of men, since almost the whole ideology amounts either to a distorted conception of this history or to a complete abstraction from it. Ideology is itself only one of the aspects of this history (Marx & Engels 1998, 34)

Leaving aside the over-generalisation, which probably they themselves were aware of anyway, there is a valid point in this determination: history, which stands for 'science' in this argument, is never free of ideology, and the study of history is, or should be, the constant endeavour to reverse the tendency to reduce the entirety of science/history to only one of its aspects.

History is not only '*his* story', to repeat the now-traditional anti-sexist intervention, but also the story of white men, the story of the European, the story of the Central Committee, and finally, the story of the history professors. Of course, every story will be shaped and framed according to the identity of the person who told it, their ideological preferences. If it were just that, however, it would be quite easy to weed these out. The childhood memories of the historiographer, their personality formation process, Oidipal obsessions, relationship with their mother and father, attitude towards the other gender, sexual orientation, homophobic/transphobic/gynophobic paranoias (if applicable), education, social position, their position in the hierarchy of 'science', their overt or covert racist/heterophobic obsessions (if applicable), all these creep into every nook and cranny of the story told. Because historiography is fundamentally an act of (re)construction. The material for this (re)construction necessarily includes the architects themselves. No story can be told without involving the narrator themselves. Perfect objectivity in this sense is nothing but an illusion. In this entire process of construction, the historiographer's personality and ideological orientation overshadow the fiction which we will later call 'history'.

Furthermore, the historiographers necessarily build upon past material, so they also have to deal with the subjectivity of documents, memoirs, testimonies, pictures, photographs, artefacts, lies, falsifications, censorship and suppression. A diplomatic meeting, a memory from the warzone, a guild's ledger, a court record, a palace gossip, a folk story, a conspiracy theory (no matter whether generated by governments or otherwise), in short, myth and 'document' and fiction and 'statistics' become mixed and embedded inseparably in the writing of history.

About a century and a half later, a sociologist/historian, Immanuel Wallerstein, comments on the ideological distortions that science ('the science of history') has to undergo in no vague terms:

> Scientists are subject to many pressures: external ones from governments, influential institutions or persons, peers, internal ones from his or her superego. We all, without exception, respond to such pressures up to a point. Furthermore, there is the Heisenberg principle writ large. The process of investigation, the procedure through which the observations are made, transforms the object of investigation. Under certain circumstances, it transforms it so much that the data obtained are quite unreliable. (Wallerstein 2004B, 16-17)

Science, or the organised/structured/systematic acts of gathering, transmitting and disseminating knowledge is never free of ideology, but it also cannot be reduced to ideology. To believe that science is a purely objective endeavour, which has a shortcut to Truth, is a dangerous illusion, which forces it closer and closer to its diametrical opposite, fundamentalist orthodoxy. To suggest that science is only one of the various narratives that make a haphazard jab at the Truth, no better or worse that Creationism, intelligent-designism, astrology or flat-earthism, is to make the Truth it seeks absolutely relative, open to whim and trivial, which accounts for the contemporary reign of Post-Truth. What we need today is an approach that could embody both, a truly ambivalent but at the same time radical attitude, which brings us to our main argument, radical ambiguity.

Radical Ambiguity

We have, then, on the one hand a political/ethical/ideological position that there already are some established, fundamental truths to be followed by all (Fundamentalism), and on the other, a position that ascertains these truths are indeed non-truths, but new ones are to be established through the use of reason and science (Enlightenment). There is, to be sure, another, third position (that of Kant in his seminal essay) that no 'truth' has the privilege to establish itself as the ultimate one, and that the concept of truth is subject to change from one generation to the other. This third position was also mentioned in our initial argument as 'nihilism', or the sceptical-agnostic outlook which refuses to take sides in the grand struggle between Fundamentalism and Enlightenment. Let us call this position that of *radical ambiguity*, and try to define it more clearly: The phrase 'radical ambiguity' seems to be an oxymoron at first sight: how can one be radical and ambiguous at the same time? If you are unsure, you are usually unable to act; radicalism, however, entails the will to act, by 'grasping things by the root'. The main question we should be asking ourselves is, what if the root itself is ambiguous, two-sided? What if there are no definite, clear-cut answers at the root, but only forks, possibilities (as should be in every self-respecting root)? Ambiguity, for one thing, is not identical with being undecided; it is an ethical position which *refuses* to be bound or delimited by a given dualism:

> An ethics of ambiguity will be one which will refuse to deny *a priori* that separate existants can, at the same time, be bound to each other, that their individual freedoms can forge laws valid for all. (de Beauvoir 1949)

Beauvoir later describes the ethical ambiguous position with reference to nihilism:

> The nihilist attitude manifests a certain truth. In this attitude one experiences the ambiguity of the human condition. But the mistake is that it defines man not as the positive existence of a lack, but as a lack at the heart of existence, whereas the truth is that existence is not a lack as such. And if freedom is experienced in this case in the form of rejection, it is not genuinely fulfilled. The nihilist is right in thinking that the world possesses no justification and that he himself is nothing. But he forgets that it is up to him to justify the world... (de Beauvoir)

Beauvoir proceeds from this argument to the statement that far from being inconsistent with one another, ambiguity and radicalism actually imply each other, that is, it is precisely the ambiguous person, equally sceptical about his/her own preconceptions and prejudices, who is more determined to take sides, to make choices and to act:

> ...[A]mbiguity is at the heart of his very attitude, for the independent man is still a man with his particular situation in the world, and what he defines as objective truth is the object of his own choice. His criticisms fall into the world of particular men. He does not merely describe. He takes sides. If he does not assume the subjectivity of his judgment, he is inevitably caught in the trap of the serious. Instead of the independent mind he claims to be, he is only the shameful servant of a cause to which he has not chosen to rally. (de Beauvoir)

In other words, the ambiguous radical is the person who is only too well aware of the fact that the hesitancy to act, the inability to take sides, makes her/him serve, willy-nilly, the cause(s) of others, those arrogant Fundamentalists of both kinds.

Let us take the controversy about abortion as an example. Although the legality of abortion is an established fact almost all over Europe and many 'Third World' countries, it is still a 'burning question' in the US, subject to much heated debate, there are even some terrorist attacks by the 'pro-lifers' on abortion clinics, and, depending on the political composition of the US Supreme Court, especially during the Trump administration when the Conservatives obtained a majority there, this legality seems to be hanging by a thread, making it extremely fragile.[4]

The positions of the 'pro-lifers' and 'pro-choicers' in the abortion controversy are clearly established. The former claim that a foetus is already a human being, and therefore abortion is murder. Judging by the policies of, e.g., the US Republican Party, however, most of these pro-lifers are also *for* the capital punishment, creating a legitimate doubt in our minds that their professed belief in the sanctity of human life might be less than candid. The latter, on the other hand, claim that giving birth is a decision that can be made only by the woman, and denying that right means contesting that woman's right to be in sole control of her own body , with which position I completely agree. Both sides seem to have valid arguments philosophically, and although we may question the sincerity of their intentions, this does not change the nature of the arguments themselves. The debate boils down to a single question: Is abortion murder? Or, more precisely, is the foetus a human being? Pro-lifers claim that they have an answer: From the moment of insemination on, the foetus is a potential human being, and although it is not yet apparent, it has a soul. The same pro-lifers may or may not be against birth control (so some may be differing from the fundamental[ist] Catholic doctrine), because *avoiding* insemination is something else altogether: God does (or may) not have a soul reserved for every copulation.

Many pro-choicers choose to argue against this position by trying to determine *when* a foetus becomes a human being, and this, unfortunately, is clearly the path of defeat. One may 'scientifically' claim that a foetus becomes a human being at a definite stage: it may be that the formation of the frontal lobes is the determining factor; another may argue that the autonomous function of the circulatory system is crucial; yet for another, it is the moment of birth itself, when the foetus ceases to be a parasitic life form on its mother's

---

[4] Even the undisputed legality of abortion 'all over Europe' is in question nowadays, with the Polish and Maltese refusal to legalise it despite the fact that it is one of the 'fundamental' tenets of the EU, and this controversy encourages the Italian conservatives to turn back and start disputing this presumably 'universal' (insofar as the universe is consisted of Europe alone) tenet.

body. Whatever 'scientific' argument you employ, you are trying to determine what makes a human being human, a philosophical and theological question which cannot be answered by scientific observation and experimentation. Marx and Engels tried a more roundabout approach in the *German Ideology* and turned the definition into a non-definition by making it self-reflexive:

> Men can be distinguished from animals by consciousness, by religion or anything else you like. They themselves begin to distinguish themselves from animals as soon as they begin to produce their means of subsistence, a step which is conditioned by their physical organization. (Marx & Engels 1998, 37)

If we try to use this argument, however, we are then confronted with the problem of defining an individual human being by self-consciousness (when they 'begin to distinguish themselves from animals'), which makes infants non-human until they are able to speak, that is, able to frame consciousness in a symbolic order. Let us face it: No one can definitely say that a foetus is not a human being. Its human-ness may be only a potentiality, and foetuses of different stages of development may represent different stages of this potentiality, so we have to accept the fact that we cannot rightly claim that pro-lifers are completely wrong, that we have the means and conceptual devices to define what makes a human being human, and *when* it makes a human being human. Then again, this does not make pro-lifers *right*. We remain ambiguous, but not undecided.

Because at this point the argument becomes one of ethics, and we have to decide whether to defend a woman's right to control her own body, indeed her destiny, or an unborn human being's right to live. I cannot positively say that a foetus is *not* human, and that aborting pregnancy is *not* murder (or at least, with an apology for the sexist term, manslaughter). There are also very serious ethical implications, however, for *outlawing* abortion, and these include the possibility of the total collapse of a woman's life, ideals, expectations, bodily integrity, indeed her entire being. The significant thing with these latter implications, however, is that, they are specified, focused; they only (at least mostly) concern women and not men, whereas the negative ethical implications of abortion have no such gender bias. I choose, therefore, the more specific and more tangible side; I choose *not to discriminate against women*, about whose humanity I have no doubt, with whom I can relate as persons, over an indiscriminate potentiality of humanity, of which I am ambiguous whether it is a mere speculation or a theological 'certainty'. And once I make my choice, I should be ready to fight for my choice; my ambiguity in no sense makes me more reticent or undecided. I am ready to fight, because I am ready to pay; if there indeed is an immortal soul, a God who provides this soul and an afterlife in which we will all be judged for our deeds, I will be paying for this choice.

The Hobgoblin of Little Minds

Let us take a seemingly less ambiguous second example, which is already implied above: probably (at least among the readers of this text) most people will agree upon the inhumanity, futility and injustice of capital punishment. Or will they? Whenever a sociopath rapes and kills a woman or a child, some people I personally know to be seriously against capital punishment undergo some kind of transformation and start to cry 'Death!' What is this mysterious element in those cases, then, that immediately transforms human beings and makes them forget about their scepticism of the state (which is supposed to execute the capital punishment), about the supposedly rehabilitative function of 'punishment' itself, and the reversibility of such punishment in case of human error? Furthermore, why does anyone still arguing against death penalty become, for these people, some kind of rapist/killers themselves, or at least an accomplice thereof?

We can observe that the rape/murder cases that are on the rise (or at least have become more visible) all around the globe recently, are not simple acts born out of wild and overwhelming sexual instincts, but rather the outcome of a masculinity that is rapidly becoming more and more fragile. This fragility, in its turn, gives way to the expression of an underlying sociopathy and psychopathy, which were there all along, but kept under check by the comfortable hegemony of privileged masculinity. Now that these privileges are eroding fast, sociopathy and psychopathy are coming to the fore and expressing themselves in overt acts of violence. Since both are deemed incurable, or even untreatable,[5] however, their expressions create in some people (that is, most of us), who mildly suffer from either but keep it under constant control by a more or less stable superego, a disproportionately furious reaction that borders on psychopathology itself, a clear case of projection.

Against this backdrop, it becomes necessary to talk about death sentence *again*, but this time from a more ambiguous position, rather than from the previous Enlightenment 'certainty' of 'right to life'. Why do we oppose the death sentence? Is it out of a universal principle that every individual has a right

---

[5] We should also consider the fact that this is not a bygone conclusion in the psychological, psychiatric and neurological communities. The majority of 'scientific' opinions on psychopathy and sociopathy mostly tend to define these two as congenital and easily diagnosable using contemporary neuro-imaging techniques, which would also lead to many *non compos mentis* defences (especially in the US courts), practically decriminalizing them. There is also a counter-argument (albeit a minority) in the same circles, which problematises this approach and argues that:

> [The] modern psychopathy research and theory – the modern version of the born criminal theory – is in a number of ways logically dubious and contingent on more than a few cultural, moral, and metaphysical assumptions. Degeneracy at the turn of the nineteenth, and psychopathy at the turn of the twenty-first centuries did not become popular because they were *supported by data*. They became popular largely *despite* the lack of compelling data. (Jalava et. al 2015, 8)

We should, therefore, even in this 'purely scientific' matter keep our ambiguity intact and not rush into the conclusion that we are dealing with monsters who deserve death at all costs.

to live, even though they themselves do not acknowledge this right in others? Even though they structurally lack empathy and compassion, with arguably no hope of reformation, and acquire *jouissance* in the pain and suffering of others? I would readily agree that *some* people may be better off dead, better for the 'common good' and even for themselves, because a life based on the suffering of others, on the impossible *jouissance* which is never satisfied but creates more need of itself every time it is attempted, is not a life worth living by any ethical standard. The question becomes, then, who will decide who these 'some' people are.

The first option that comes to mind, of course, is the legal system. That system, however, needs generalised basic rules and principles to make this decision, and these rules and principles always lag behind (sometimes *decades* behind) scientific research. If left alone, the state and the legal system it entails prefer, first and foremost, to define crimes against itself as 'major crimes' and give priority to 'punishing' these, roughly follow the guidelines established by millennia of patriarchy and class-rule in other offences, and occasionally kowtow to public opinion in case of a particularly violent crime that upsets communal conscience and make an example of such every once in a while, to placate 'public outrage'. It is obvious that this legal system cannot be trusted with an irrevocable and permanent 'remedy' such as capital punishment, because if it were, any radical oppositional stance against the system would be facing mortal peril, while psychopaths and sociopaths would constantly fall through the cracks of the system which is mainly concerned with its own survival and little else.

Sociopathy and psychopathy, on the other hand, may be congenital (then again, they may not), as many genetic and behavioural scientists believe, and if they are right, that is, if it is embedded in the genetic structure, there may be no hope of a cure, and even treatment may only be suppressing the symptoms for a definite period. We may, therefore, perhaps trust the medical profession or the science of psychology to make the decision for us. Or can we? Aren't we painfully aware that psychiatric and psychological diagnosis and treatment have been subject to serious criticism for a long time from, for instance, Laing and Szasz from within the profession to, for instance, Foucault and Deleuze from a philosophical stance? All this criticism indicates that both medicine and the science of psychology are severely conflicted areas of knowledge; they are both adversely influenced (even manipulated) by the pharmacological industry from without and positivistic arrogance and orthodoxy from within, and hence matters of life and death cannot be left to psychologists and psychiatrists alone.

So we are back at where we started: we cannot decide what to do with murderous sociopaths and psychopaths, and many among us, even those most critical with the existing political and legal structure, suddenly become willing to trust the state with this decision (and its execution), just in order to satisfy their thirst for revenge. Since it is not a *personal* revenge (most of them do not even *know* the victims), we wouldn't be very much off the mark if we doubted their sincerity. They want a dangerous sociopath dead for his crime, dangerous because we have every reason to believe they will repeat it given the slightest chance, but they do not want to do it themselves; they want to *delegate* somebody else to do it: the judges, the jury, the executioners, the lawmakers, the police, anybody. They want to delegate not only *the act of killing* itself, but also the uncertainty of deciding whether the accused is really guilty, if so whether they are really irreformable, incurable. They want, in short, to delegate the act of *telling the truth* (not only of speaking it out loud, but also of telling it from the false) to an impersonal agency (the state and its legal edifice) without a sense of ethics but only with a set of fixed, unnegotiable rules.

Foucault reminds us that there is a path to Truth, which is *speaking it out loud*. He uses the classical Greek term (*parrhesia*) for telling the truth, and calls the persons who engage in it *parrhesiastes* (truth-teller). If you tell your opinion in sincerity, you are also 'telling the truth':

> The *parrhesiastes* is not only sincere and says what is his opinion, but his opinion is also the truth. He says what he knows to be true. The second characteristic of *parrhesia*, then, is that there is always an exact coincidence between belief and truth. (Foucault 2001, 14)

'Wait,' one is bound to exclaim, 'isn't this what you were arguing against all along? How does one's opinion become the truth just by proclaiming it?' Well, there is a lot of small print under Foucault's 'exact coincidence between belief and truth', and we should read it before we hastily agree or disagree with him. One of the most important preconditions he specifies for *parrhesia* is *courage*:

> *Parrhesia*, then, is linked to courage in the face of danger: it demands the courage to speak the truth in spite of some danger. And in its extreme form, telling the truth takes place in the 'game' of life or death. (Foucault 2001, 16)

It is not sufficient to proclaim your opinion for it to become the truth, you have to risk something, probably your life in speaking it out loud. The opinions, therefore, of all kinds of sycophants and toadies inhabiting a close-knit circle around the autocrats and would-be autocrats (elected or otherwise) of our day, around, say, Trump or Modi, Johnson or Bolsonaro, Putin or Erdoğan, are not *truth* or anything that comes close to it. Whether they do it privately or publicly, in the mainstream or new media, around or within official circles, they do not risk anything in voicing these opinions; quite to the contrary they either gain something for doing it, or, worse still, they are *commissioned* to do it, hence they are not *parrhesiastes*. A *parrhesiastes* is the one who proclaims *this*:

> [...] singing only has meaning
> when it pulses in the veins

of someone who will
die singing truths that are real. (Victor Jara 1973, *Manifiesto*)

… and is killed while singing it the year he recorded it. To be willing to die for your beliefs does not, however, always imply that you are *parrhesiastes,* especially in the case of suicide bombers. Quite to the contrary, the suicide bomber is almost the reverse of *parrhesiastes,* because they first decide to commit suicide, and then kill other people in doing so: they do not *risk* anything, because they have already given up their life *before the act.* In suicide there are no consequences; *Parrhesia* is speaking what you believe to be the truth and then suffering the consequences, whatever they may be. Marx wrote to Ruge in September 1843:

> But, if constructing the future and settling everything for all times are not
> our affair, it is all the more clear what we have to accomplish at present: I
> am referring to *ruthless criticism* of all that exists, ruthless both in the sense of
> not being afraid of the results it arrives at and in the sense of being just as
> little afraid of conflict with the powers that be.' (Marx 1843 [2010]).

Not being afraid of what our ruthless criticism, that is, the truth we tell, may entail is two-fold: it is not being afraid of what may befall us through the acts of those in power whose wrath we may invoke, but it is also not being afraid of the possible conflicts with our allies, friends, our past statements, convictions or positions, our own ideologies. It is about embracing ambiguity, but remaining radical at the same time.

In the same vein, opinions uttered from a position of political power, or from offices sanctioned or commissioned by this power are not *parrhesia* either:

> It is because the *parrhesiastes* must take a risk in speaking the truth that the
> king or tyrant generally cannot use *parrhesia*; for *he* risks nothing. (Foucault
> 2001, 16)

The state, or its representatives cannot be *parrhesiastes.* A judge, a prosecutor or a jury cannot be *parrhesiastes, unless* the prosecutor investigates somebody in power, or the jury or the judge decide against the directives or interests of the powers that be. If a jury or a judge convict somebody following the letter (rather than the spirit) of the law in order to appease the powers that be, or some public opinion or outrage, this is not *parrhesia*. If a person speaks out loud about a heinous crime, demands the worst punishment possible, death, but delegates it to somebody else, the prosecutor, the jury, the judge, the executioner, this is not *parrhesia*. This is cowardice, plain and simple.

In conclusion, I do not necessarily defend the incurable sociopaths' and psychopaths' 'right to live' when I oppose the death penalty. They may have deserved to die. Of course, I may be accused of inconsistency for doing so, but thankfully Ralph Waldo Emerson has already spoken in my defence: 'A foolish consistency is the hobgoblin of little minds, adored by little statesmen and philosophers and divines. With consistency a great soul has simply nothing to do.' (Emerson 2004, 44) I do not claim to be a 'great soul' (that declaration of grandeur belongs to Emerson alone), but only an ambiguous soul, who sacrifices a petty consistency in order to remain radical: I am *against* the death penalty, but I may (depending on the circumstances and a further clarification in theory) defend killing such sociopaths and psychopaths, if you can make yourself commit that act. If you are certain of your facts; if, for instance, you catch them during the act, or the accused actually confess, even boast of their crimes. If you kill them and be willing to suffer the consequences (including the probability to be proven wrong in the long run), then you become a *parrhesiastes*, and maybe receive a standing ovation from me. By 'consequences' of course, I do not only mean going to jail, or maybe being sentenced to death yourself, but also being reconciled to the fact that you have become a murderer yourself and you will have to live with it for the rest of your life. Would I have done the thing I suggest myself? Maybe, especially if I caught one of these murderers during the act. But then I would take responsibility for my act and would not cry 'mitigating circumstances', because nothing can mitigate the fact that I have taken a life: there is no middle way here, even when you are ambiguous. As Yoda would have said: Do, or do not, there is no [delegate].

The Case of Armenian Genocide

My last example will be the much-discussed case of the 1915-18 massacre of Ottoman Armenians by the Ottoman state.[6] To be perfectly candid, I am no expert historian on this event, and my knowledge is limited to the findings and claims of others (be they Turkish, Armenian or 'disinterested' third parties) who pretend to be so. As far as I have learned from the studies of trusted colleagues, in 1915, the leaders of the *Ittihat ve Terakki* Party, then in power in the Ottoman Empire, decided that the Armenians living in the Empire should be forcibly deported. Their excuse was that the Armenians living close to the Russian border were cooperating with Russia, then at war with the Ottoman Empire, with the hope of establishing their independence, and therefore, the argument went, this action was taken in self-defence. The problem with this excuse is that, most of the deportees were from other parts of the Empire, some as far from the Russian border as Istanbul and Edirne. Furthermore, the Armenians were being deported to a non-existent place, that is, their destination did not have the facilities to support even a tenth of the population that was being moved. As a result, at least hundreds of thousands perished on the road, some as a result of starvation, but most as a result of attacks by paramilitary gangs.

---

[6] This event was named by the Armenians themselves as *Medz Yeghern* (The Great Calamity). The international debate about 'Genocide' came much later, when a case was being made in international courts and international conscience, since a more familiar catchphrase was needed. I prefer to use the original Armenian phrase, for reasons I will try to elucidate below.

These are the 'historical facts' as far as I am concerned.

The excuse that the deportation was an act of self-defence, and Armenian gangs were also sacking and massacring Turkish villages, does not hold water for me, because there is concrete evidence that the deportation was more of a planned action rather than a self-defence reflex, and in any case, the measures taken were colossally disproportionate with the alleged threat. Having said all this, I would still be under the threat of a jail sentence in Switzerland and in France, because I do not *unconditionally* call this historical event 'genocide'. Of course, I have some specific reasons for carefully refraining from using this particular term, reasons which do not seem to disturb Swiss and French legislators in the slightest. In the ultimate instance, however, they (pretend they) *know*, and I am *ambiguous*, so they must be unequivocally right. Surely, they would be surprised that anyone who can read or write can be ambiguous about this 'clear and undisputable fact'.

For others of the same Enlightenment creed, however, the massacre of Sétif and Guelma by the French in May 8 1945, may be considered 'clearly and indisputably' a 'genocide'. For still others, the forcible transportation of Africans from 17th through 19th centuries to the Americas, a state-sanctioned act in most European countries, may constitute 'clearly and indisputably' an act of 'genocide', since most of these Africans had died on the way and at their destination, in the cotton and tobacco fields. And of course, the almost total annihilation of Native American nations, first by colonizing European states and later by the USA, may very possibly be considered a case of 'genocide'.

I am not trying to claim that those who are very self-righteously insistent upon the 'fact' of 'Armenian Genocide' should keep quiet in a pact of silence of the guilty, since their hands are no cleaner than those of the rulers of the Ottoman Empire. What I'm trying to ascertain is that, although in each of these cases there is not a shred of doubt about the savagery, inhumanity and injustice of the act, the use of the term 'genocide' is determined by political or diplomatic, rather than humanitarian or historical considerations, and the present-day use of the term 'genocide' is a lame attempt by the powers-that-be, to *retain* the rights of the existing and internationally legitimised nation-states to exercise coercion and violence on their subjects on the one hand, and to try to keep these acts of violence within the limits of an artificially created 'international conscience' on the other.

The Holocaust, or the *Shoah* as it was called by the victims of that insurmountable act of inhumanity, was a perfect excuse for the creation of this artificial conscience, because the alleged violator was, for a transitory period, a 'non-state', so to speak, in a state of *total defeat* (something very rarely seen in our history of wars and massacres), and therefore, anything done to belittle, intimidate and emasculate this political entity was possible for a definite period of time. This is why the Trial at Nuremberg was an actual possibility at that time, taken seriously by almost everyone, while in our day similar trials for international war crimes and genocides are both much more complicated and taken less seriously, except, maybe, for the trial of Slobodan Milošević. Even the trials (and 'executions') of Saddam and Qaddafi were more farcical and, in the end more pathetic, leaving much for doubt in the victors' haste for 'getting it done with' to the point of lynching (in Qaddafi's case), although almost nobody actually sympathised with these two strongmen, both mass-murderers in their own right.

The internationally sanctioned concept of Genocide is the expression of a carefully calculated halfway point between the need for pacifying the universal outrage against state-sanctioned atrocities against especially precarious subjects of that state, and the need for all states to retain the power and privilege to repeat these atrocities in the future should the need arose. The solution was to isolate what the Nazi state did during the second great war, to package it as a specific act against a group of people defined as an ethnic/religious minority, and carefully denounce it as an act against a specific ethnicity, carefully and covertly leaving open the possibility to repeat the same act against, say, ideological, political, gender and sexual orientation minorities. None of these groups constitute a *genus* by its proper definition, so putting, say, gays in concentration camps, which the Nazis actually did, or killing political opponents by the hundreds of thousands, like Pol Pot did in Cambodia in the 70s, are not genocides *per se*. These atrocities could be named, to be sure, 'Genocides' *after the fact*, but this does not help in any way to avoid them, and creates confusion as to the definition of the act, just like, for instance, the confusion created by calling Islamophobia a kind of *racism*. Islam, as we all know, is not a *race*, and therefore Islamophobia *is not racism*, although it is no better or no more justifiable and/or excusable.[7]

I would like to point out, at this juncture, that I would hate to be mistaken for somebody who denies, or even argues, the reality (for me, *the Real*) of the Holocaust or the *Shoah*. It was the ultimate act of deliberate and systematic inhumanity, savagery and cruelty directed against a *specific group of people*. The emphasis on *race* in the Holocaust, however, still needs to be problematised: What the Holocaust shows us is not only the extremes a nation-state may go against one of its subject nationalities, but the extremes a nation-state can go

---

[7] We should, at this point in history, start to distinguish between different forms of hate and animosity against various 'others', and stop dumping them under a single name. Not every authoritarian/autocratic regime that emerges from allegedly 'democratic' elections and eventually abolishes the latter is 'fascism' or Nazism. These two were the outcomes of very specific historical and politico-economic circumstances, and not every regime that resembles them should be named so. In the same vein, not every ideology of hate and animosity towards others is *racism*. Racism is only one of these ideologies, and, say, Islamophobia, homophobia, gynophobia, transphobia, and many other 'phobias' do not deserve to be categorised (and, albeit unintentionally, *trivialised*) under the umbrella term, racism. If we still need an umbrella term, why not try *Heterophobia*, fear/hate of *others*, and restore the honour of the much-abused Greek word '*heteros*' (other, different) in the same stroke?

against its subjects, period. The emphasis on race (and hence on the term 'genocide') only serves to particularise and therefore hide the immense powers of coercion and violence accumulated by modern states vis-à-vis their subjects, and the pitiful and still diminishing powers of self-defence of these subjects vis-à-vis their respective states. When you call such an act a 'genocide', it immediately becomes consoling and even comforting for ethnic majorities everywhere, who themselves occupy precarious positions vis-à-vis the state for *reasons other than race*: it can only happen to *others*, not us! Alas, it can happen to all of us, everywhere, regardless of nation, religion, skin colour and gender. Hence my reluctance, my ambiguity to use the term 'genocide'.

However, with my insistence on ambiguity, I would be no luckier with the authorities in Turkey, where the denial of the events of 1915 is official policy, because I would certainly use the term 'genocide' *in Turkey* which would lead to my being brought before justice there as well*,* because this is the only way I can speak the truth, and become a *parrhesiastes*.

Whether there actually *was* a genocide is not the main issue here, because calling that terrible massacre, that 'Great Calamity' *–Medz Yeghern* as it was named by its victims— a genocide or not, does not in any sense diminish or aggravate the inhumanity of the act. In Switzerland and France I would emphasise the evidence that tends to indicate that 'genocide' in the politico-legal sense of the term does not do justice to the act itself, in order to problematise the concept and to unveil the motives behind the self-righteous and holier-than-thou attitude of the legislators there; while in Turkey I would do exactly the opposite, in order to challenge the feeble attempts at cover-up by Turkish governments for more than a hundred years, so that the founding ideological structure of the Turkish Republic can also be problematised. And if in another court (let's say in the hypothetical court of European 'intellectual conscience') I would be charged with inconsistency, I would again quote Emerson.

Ambiguity without Hypocrisy

The emphasis on ambiguity usually raises doubts about the sincerity of the ambiguous subject. Maintaining a constantly ambiguous attitude on every issue, in order to problematise the presumably immutable truisms and the taken-for-granted dualities calcified around it, is indeed impossible for the singular/unique subject. As a result, they, in actual reality, don't. I don't live in France, Turkey, Iran, Switzerland and the US simultaneously, so my attitude towards, let's say, abortion, goes unnoticed here in Turkey, where it is legal. In the same vein, when I talk about the Armenian Genocide here, I am utterly unconvincing for Turkish nationalists (even the milder, well-meaning ones), because my claim that I would have refrained from using the term in Switzerland goes untested. The Kemalists knowingly smile at me when I stand for the right of women to cover here, because they know that my statement that I would do (or would have done) exactly the opposite in Iran or Saudi Arabia is merely a claim, because I don't usually travel to these countries for activities of personal political protest. When in 2020, US drones kill an Iranian general, Soleimani, who is responsible for numerous civilian deaths including many Kurds, taking an ambiguous position, not only condemning him for these deaths, but also the US for committing an obvious war crime, for carrying out a 'hit' on Iraqi soil, may mean something ethically, but not politically, because I neither live in the US to actively demonstrate against this war crime, nor I had lived in Iran to actively oppose the crimes committed by Soleimani himself. Similarly, during the US invasion of Iraq in 2003, the radical ambiguous position that the USA and Saddam were 'both worse' (Žižek 1999) did not hold water, because we were not in Iraq actively opposing Saddam in the years preceding the invasion.

We have to ask ourselves the notoriously Leninist question then: What is to be done? It is perfectly obvious that, although the radical ambiguous attitude sounds like a mere statement of personal ethics *prima facie*, it is neither (only) ethical nor (only) personal. Furthermore, as long as it remains that way, it immediately becomes, or at least sounds, hypocritical, regardless of intention. One possible answer lies in a redefinition of the subject who is supposed to be radically ambiguous: It is definitely not a *singular*, individual subject, for, although we are pretty sure that no individual subject represents a unity (in the sense that it is *barred*, that is, both divided and prohibited), it is nevertheless restricted to a singular spatial and temporal continuum. It does not have the ability to occupy more than its share of space and time, so it cannot ambiguate any issue at hand, other than positing two (or more) seemingly conflicting statements one after the other.

The individual subject can be ambiguous, or it can be radical, but it cannot be both. It cannot radicalise its ambiguous position, and it cannot ambiguate (problematise, question and sublate) its radical stand, other than merely theoretically, in the realm of pure thought. It cannot, on the other hand, assume the Universalist stand characteristic of the Enlightenment thinking and claim to be a *universal*, totalizing subject, in which case it will cease to be ambiguous. The only subject with a rightful claim to radical ambiguity is a *particular* subject, a defined plurality rather than a singularity, both a subject, therefore, and made up of interacting subjects, and a part (*party*) rather than an assumed whole, that is, a subject among subjects. This particular subject cannot be anything else than a *party*, both in the political sense of the word, as in a social/political *movement*, and in the sense that it is a *party* to something. It has to be *trans*national (rather than *inter*national, which assumes the national entities instead of trying to sublate them); so that synchronous *passages à l'acte* within multiple national/local entities while maintaining the ambiguous position will be possible. More than twenty years ago, Žižek, in his article on the NATO bombing of Belgrade, had characterised the task of constructing these transnational subjects as 'the only serious question today':

> [The] alternative between the New World Order and the neo-racist nationalists opposing it is a false one: these are the two sides of the same coin — the New World Order itself breeds monstrosities that it fights. [...] The way to fight the capitalist New World Order is not by supporting local proto-Fascist resistances to it, but to focus on the only serious question today: how to build transnational political movements and institutions strong enough to seriously constrain the unlimited rule of the capital... (Žižek 1999)

The creation of such transnational political movements will not only render visible the fact that global capitalism already includes and constantly breeds the local fundamentalist resistances against it, but also allow for the possibility that the ambiguous position vis-à-vis the dichotomies created by this situation, the refusal 'to take sides' in practical dilemmas like 'NATO vs. ISIS', 'International Community vs. Assad', 'US vs. Taliban', 'US vs. Iran', is itself a viable political 'side'. This side, which can only result in inaction and eventually in a cynical attitude if taken by singular individual subjects, will become politically and practically viable if taken by a multinational, particular subject, in the sense that it will construct *a third party* above and beyond the 'poor freedom either to accept or reject', or the 'referendum'[8] offered us by global capitalism.

It must be emphasised, however, that these 'transnational political subjects' are not the same thing as issue-based transnational *institutions* like Greenpeace, Amnesty International or *Médecins Sans Frontières*, because, although these institutions must and do involve in local and international politics most of the time, they are not political institutions *per se*, in the sense that their area of interest and activity is usually limited to a single issue. The transnational 'social forums' that have emerged from the (formerly anti-) alter-globalization movements of Seattle and Genoa in early 90s, on the other hand, suffer no such limitation. The same thing is even truer for the 'Occupy' movements of the 2010s, the Gezi movement in Istanbul in 2013, even for the 'Arab Spring' of the same era, although not with the desired result most of the time. These events constitute *inter-subjective loci*, rather than transnational subjects in and of themselves, but these loci (Zucotti Park, Gezi Park and Tahrir Square, like Tiananmen back in 1989), in their symbolic significance, clear the ground for further cooperation, coordination and solidarity for the decades to come. The

---

[8] I take this concept of 'referendum' from Roland Barthes' definition of 'readerly texts', in which the reader is presented a two-way choice, of either accepting or rejecting: 'This reader is thereby plunged into a kind of idleness – he is intransitive; he is, in short, serious: instead of functioning himself, instead of gaining access to the magic of the signifier, to the pleasure of writing, he is left with no more than the poor freedom either to accept or reject the text: reading is nothing more than a referendum. Opposite the writerly text, then, is its counter-value, its negative, reactive value: what can be read, but not written: the readerly. We call any readerly text a classic text.' (*S/Z*, 4)

first indication that this new wave is imminent is the Extinction Rebellion, not an institutionalised and issue-based organisation like Greenpeace, but a properly transnational, trans-generational and multi-focal event on a world scale. The fact that the apparent symbolic spearhead of this continuing event is a 'leader who is not a leader', a teenager, Greta Thunberg, with no ideological predispositions or political agenda, is proof enough that it is indeed 'a historical movement going on under our very eyes' (Marx & Engels 1848 [2010]).

Le Sujet Supposé Savoir

Any transnational entity with a claim to radical political action is, or quickly and willy-nilly becomes, a 'subject who is supposed to know'. The problem, or rather, the discrepancy here is that supposition and fact do not correspond, at least not entirely. Any practical/political action (even abstention) is a call to other subjects, either for collaboration and cooperation, or as a challenge. In either case, the subject is supposed to know: it is supposed to know the circumstances surrounding the issue, its extent, its history, and its transnational and historical implications. Furthermore, the moment such a subject is politicised, it has to act as if it knows what it is talking about, that is, as if it is not ambiguous. In short, it is exactly in the same position with the psychoanalyst in Lacan's definition: the psychoanalyst is supposed (by the analysand) to know the secret behind their symptoms, their character, their complexes and neuroses, while it is a physical impossibility for such knowledge to exist. The psychoanalyst does not (or should not) have a claim to such knowledge, however; it is only the analysand's assumption that they do. As a matter of fact, the entire process of psychoanalysis is a series of disillusionments experienced by the analysand with the ultimate realization that their analyst does not know. As the insight of the analysand grows and their self-knowledge increases, the supposition that the analyst is an omniscient subject begins to fade. By the time a successful analysis is terminated, the analyst must have been demoted, if not to the status of a total ignoramus, but at least to an equal footing with the analysand, not in matters of psychoanalytical understanding, but with regard to the inherent 'problems' of the analysand. For this process to be successful, however, the analyst must constantly be aware of the fact that they do not know. According to Lacan, therefore, the entire process of psychoanalytical therapy is dominated by the constant tension between the analysand's supposition that the analyst knows, and the analyst's awareness that they don't.

As can easily be seen, the main threat to a successful therapy comes not from the analysand's refusal to suppose that the analyst knows (in which case they will eventually abandon analysis and seek help elsewhere), but from the analyst's failure to accept their lack of knowledge. It is always easier to boast a non-existent surplus than to accept an actual lack humbly. Most unsuccessful, unduly protracted or aborted psychoanalytic therapies have failed due to the inability of the analyst to accept that they are not omniscient.

The same thing applies to radical political subjects, with a vengeance: The Jacobins in the French Revolution and the Bolsheviks in the Russian Revolution were subjects who were supposed to know, and the moment they started to share this supposition with their followers, they turned into conservatives, into radical fundamentalists, so to speak. People follow, vote for, or actually fight for a political party, when they believe that that party knows what it is doing, with a coherent political agenda and a firm ethical footing (i.e., it doesn't lie to its followers). The method to endorse this supposition may vary: It may be anything ranging from successful propaganda to boldly telling the truth, from demagoguery to mass psychological manipulation, from meticulous public relations to a science-fictional mind-control. It does not matter. The real danger, however, lies not in the fact that the 'masses' may (mis?)place their trust in a party who doesn't actually 'know', but in the precise moment that party starts to believe that it actually knows.

The way to avoid this transformation, from *le sujet qui supposé savoir* (the subject who is supposed to know) to *le sujet qui suppose qu'il sais* (the subject who supposes it knows), is not merely good intentions, or an oath to stay ambiguous. For one thing, any radical political entity in history that has succeeded *not* in seizing and holding onto political power, but managed to retain the trust of the masses, has built-in self-ambiguating mechanisms. The least of these mechanisms is the right of minority opinions to survive and speak out within and from within this entity, so that the mass of people, which is by no means a unified, consolidated entity but made up of a myriad of conflicting ideas, opinions, interests and issues, may feel more or less represented most of the time. This is not because such an entity should feel compelled to conform to an abstract democratic ideal due to an ethical commitment, but because this is the only rational way to acknowledge the fact that the revolutionary subject is indeed a barred/split subject (**$**), a subject that is not only prohibited by the symbolic order, since that order is structured to exclude any factor that threatens to upset or subvert its integrity, its stranglehold on 'truth', but also it is split, divided, *not-one*. The homogenizing drive toward unification is the fundamental danger facing the revolutionary subject, and in order to save itself from itself, it should take every possible measure to remain divided. Marx and Engels' insistence that the communists are *only one of the parties of the working class, with no sectarian or separate principles of their own,* indicates that they were well aware of this danger: For them the only revolutionary subject was the working class itself, which is not a homogenous, undivided subject at all, but a composite subject made up of parts ('parties'), only one of which is the communists.

It is possible to state that the claim to positive knowledge or an unshakeable faith, and the belief that one (be this 'one' a single individual, a political entity, a whole nation or indeed 'universal humanity') is a homogenous, unified subject, are only different aspects of the same thing. By claiming possession of positive knowledge or unshakeable faith, one is also making a bid to being a unified subject, a non-self-contradictory entity, which seems to be the only way to escape confusion, uncertainty and doubt in a world where 'truth' seems to be more and more out of reach. The insistence on positive knowledge is a desperate attempt to be and remain yourself: you can only know, if there is an undivided subject who knows it knows.

The Cartesian progress from doubt to certainty, from the suspicion that there exists an 'evil demon' who constantly deceives me to believe that there is a world out there when there is not, to the certainty of the existence of God, necessarily supposes, *en passant*, the certainty of the existence of an 'I' which is a unified subject. Most Oriental philosophies, on the other hand, from Zoroastrianism[9] to Daoism, from Zen Buddhism to *Tasavvuf*, tentatively accept the co-existence of both (the 'Evil Demon' and God) as complementary possibilities rather than absolutes at war with each other, a war in which only one will prevail in the end, so the 'I' always remains divided.

The insistence on positive knowledge or moral certainty and the disavowal of ambiguity, then, are only different expressions of an appeal (indeed a plea) for inclusion in the symbolic order, a supplication for forgiveness and (re)approval by the Name-of-the-Father[10], who would appreciate my being in this world and lend meaning to my existence. By *knowing*, (through faith or through science) we are in fact crying '*Pater, peccavi!*': *Forgive me Father, for I have sinned by doubting, but now I know*. In order to be able to confess (or make a 'self-criticism' in the officially approved Maoist manner), you should know what sin is, and that you have sinned, that is, you should already have analysed and made peace with yourself. Most of the time this peace is through rationalisation, submission or conformity rather than a genuine insight, but who cares? By *knowing*, the subject goes beyond ethics, the way the Crusades, the Jihad Fighters, the *Hashashin*, the Auto-Da-Fé have gone, and the Jacobins, the Bolsheviks and most revolutions after them have eventually ended up in. Knowing-too-well is also submitting ourselves to a supposedly higher moral authority, that of the Name-of-the-Father, hence absolving us from all responsibility. This is how we can, in a clean conscience, execute a death sentence, become a suicide bomber, blow up Twin Towers, invade Iraq,

---

[9] One of the possible etymological roots of the term 'Zarathustra' is old Persian *zaratuštra*, which means 'perhaps'.

[10] 'Name-of-the Father' is Lacan's name for the symbolic presence of a 'father' which may or may not be 'there' bodily, in whose gaze we constantly try to legitimise our existence. Depending on the culture we live in, the father may already be dead, left, emasculated, or has been replaced by a god, God, the state, the King, the police, anything or anybody representing authority and domination. It is the entryway for us to the Symbolic Order, language, the only structured existence to offer us meaning and order instead of chaos. When we disavow it completely, we cannot connect to a meaningful world; when we submit to it completely, we give up any claim to freedom and independence—remember Dostoevsky's imaginary dialogue between Jesus Christ and Tomas de Torquemada?

Afghanistan or Rojava, forbid or promote this or that ideology or act, commit genocide or suicide, take revenge or torture.

We should not, on the other hand, delude ourselves with the utopian fiction that remaining ambiguous protects us from doing any or all of these. A radically ambiguous stance is not a guarantee against all the perils and traps that radical movements, policies or persons have been subjected to throughout history. It is only an insight, an awareness that our (radical) actions will not ever be sanctioned or endorsed by a higher authority, a 'big Other', and that we should always act with the knowledge that we will always be responsible for our choices and actions. As radically ambiguous subjects we will always be trespassers and transgressors; we will always be accountable, if not to a higher authority, then to our own ethos. We will never be given the 'right' to state, or act in the name of, a Truth, unless we create that Truth by boldly uttering it and acting upon this utterance, without 'being afraid of the results it arrives at and in the sense of being just as little afraid of conflict with the powers that be.' A radically ambiguous subject is never permitted to do anything, so it never asks for permission. Whatever we choose to do or not do, we should never allow a 'higher authority' to compel us to do (or not do) it: the Name-of-the-Father may still invite us in the neatly ordered cosmos of language, the symbolic order, and we may heed this call; but it is up to us whether to allow it to determine and guide our every step in that order: we, as human beings, must have reached the maturity to be accountable for our existence, otherwise we rightly deserve extinction. If we forgo this maturity, we become passive members of Torquemada's flock, Nazism's innocent onlookers, any autocrat's silent sycophants, or a collaborator during or after the fact in every act of murder, rape and torture, unifying in the same, enormous guilt. A radically ambiguous stance may be our only hope in this world which is dangerously approaching ultimate unification and consequently, annihilation.

CHAPTER 2

THE MIDAS BLESSING

TURNING COMMODITIES INTO GIFTS

Books, you know, they're not just commodities. The profit motive often is in conflict with the aims of art. We live in capitalism. Its power seems inescapable. So did the divine right of kings. Any human power can be resisted and changed by human beings. Resistance and change often begin in art, and very often in our art— the art of words.

[...] We who live by writing and publishing want –and should demand– our fair share of the proceeds. But the name of our beautiful reward is not profit.

Its name is freedom.

Ursula Le Guin, National Book Award Acceptance Speech, 2014

But is not the gift, if there is any, also that which interrupts economy? That which, in suspending economic calculation, no longer gives rise to exchange? That which opens the circle so as to defy reciprocity or symmetry, the common measure, and so as to turn aside the return in view of the no-return? [...] It must not circulate, it must not be exchanged, it must not in any case be exhausted, as a gift, by the process of exchange, by the movement of circulation of the circle in the form of return to the point of departure. If the figure of the circle is essential to economics, the gift must remain *uneconomic*. Not that it remains foreign to the circle, but it must keep a relation of foreignness to the circle, a relation without relation of familiar foreignness.

Jacques Derrida, *Given Time*, 1991

Žižek had already stated in 2008, that one of the irresolvable conflicts of contemporary capitalism was centred on 'intellectual property': 'The inadequacy of private property for so called "intellectual property." The key antagonism of the new (digital) industries is thus: how to maintain the form of (private) property, within which the logic of profit can be maintained?' (Žižek 2008, 422) The antagonism he is referring to is a properly Marxian one, between 'the forces of production', that is, the digital technology of the internet allowing for universal sharing, free of market pressures, and 'the relations of production', that is, private property posturing as 'intellectual property'. Free sharing of digitally reproducible works of art and thought on the internet is the most serious challenge that capitalist forms of property had to face ever, and the only 'rational'' measure capitalism can imagine is an unequivocally dystopian control of the internet, as can be observed in the legal steps taken in the US and other Western countries, as opposed to the more arbitrary ('totalitarian') measures taken in China, Iran, India, Turkey, etc. The problem with these legal steps is that, they are no less totalitarian than the internet regime in China, however hard the US, UK and EU authorities try to rationalise it.

We have, then, come to a crossroads, a sort of a Y junction, between free and universal sharing, a massively utopian endeavour, and totalitarian control, the dystopian way out. It is not, however, a simple fight between the forces of good and evil, between supposedly free souls and the bogey of 'capitalism': The utopian endeavour or horizon is both imminent and immanent, and it is up to all of us to make the decision, to make the choice between utopia and dystopia. Are we, especially as thinkers, writers, artists and academics, we who engage in the 'magic of the signifier' as Barthes would have called it, willing to let existing governments protect our property at whatever cost, in order to retain our present status as small property owners, or are we going to give up our little island of privilege in order to share what we have to offer freely with everyone, everywhere. Utopia (or dystopia) starts here and now in this simple but far-reaching choice.

'Intellectual Property'

As usual, Science Fiction had been aware of it much before, but mainstream popular culture started predicting a virtual utopia through the World Wide Web as soon as the name 'internet' was coined. Again, as usual, Science Fiction was much more ambiguous about the prospect of computers ('machines') combining their power; and as a result, predictions of utopia and dystopia in SF went hand in hand, the dystopic ones going as far back as E. M. Forster's 'The Machine Stops' in 1909.

Popular culture rarely shares (serious) Science Fiction's studied wariness and learned paranoia: any new and path-breaking scientific or technological advance (or at least the advertisement thereof) is enough cause for seemingly endless celebration in the media, albeit for a short while. So was the case with the internet. Even before the age of perpetual googling, Facebook, Twitter, Instagram and Wikipedia (not to mention Wikileaks), everybody was sure that knowledge had finally become free for all. And since 'Knowledge [was] power,' power was also to be universally shared. Or would be. Or would be in a short while, just wait...

As usual, popular culture was wrong, especially on two very important counts. The first mistake was the almost automatic identification of knowledge with information. As a matter of fact, the internet was true to its promise of actually making much information almost universally available, but to what end? Information is chaotic in itself, and, as all faithful library-goers, members of that almost extinct species, know, even the greatest and richest library on earth is almost totally useless without an intelligible cataloguing system. Knowledge is the art of relating, combining and integrating otherwise useless bits of information, and digital media, now universalised through the WWW, was (and still is) far from offering us *knowledge*; this remains something each one of us has to discover for ourselves.

Even this argument, however, is too philosophical and academic, if we consider the situation we are in today, which brings us to my second argument against the 'self-evident' utopian nature of the internet. As David M. Berry and Giles Moss remark in the Introduction to their *Libre Culture* (2008):

> There is an important tension between:
> 1. Public access to information and knowledge in a public domain.
> 2. Private ownership of information and knowledge.

> No matter how much you try to square these basic liberal principles, they are in direct contradiction to each other. And whilst property was based on physical items at least there could be trade offs that some societies would accept and try to regulate the effects through the welfare state (e.g. political equality versus economic inequality). However when information and knowledge are privatised, the very preconditions of a critical public required within a democratic society are denied to that public (Giles & Moss, 2008, 2-3).

This argument brings to the fore a crucial question as to the essential nature of the internet: is the internet an *agora*, a free arena of meeting, interaction and sharing for all free citizens (and since we are not living in Ancient Greece, this is supposed to mean all of us), or is it merely a disguised, glorified and digitised *marketplace*, where commodities are bought and sold with a modicum of polite (and more often than not, not-so-polite) interaction in between? The answer should be, it is *not only* an agora, *but also* a marketplace, and since these two features are always in a strained and uneasy coexistence, each one takes over some (and more often than not, the worst) characteristics of the other, and this makes the situation even more complex: the free-sharing agora sometimes becomes an unchecked arena of misinformation, lies and conspiracy theories, easy and baseless judgements, something taken over from the capitalist 'free market'; and the marketplace turns all personal and supposedly private information shared in the agora into commodities and sells them to the highest bidder for economic, and often political, gain.[1]

---

[1] The Facebook-Cambridge Analytica Scandal of 2018 was (as yet) the pinnacle of such acts, when

There is no doubt that information and knowledge are indeed/already commodities, since we spend a considerable portion of our lives buying them, throughout our so-called 'education', and, if some of us prefer to remain in the academic community, we work for the establishments (be they public or private) that specialise in selling them. Furthermore, most products of intellectual and artistic endeavour can be classified as 'information' or 'knowledge' at one point or another, and from the beginnings of the capitalist mode of production onwards, they have also been treated as commodities, and their 'creators' as petty commodity producers or workers. Daniel Defoe who is usually credited with being the first English Novelist *per se*, was acutely aware of this fact when he wrote in the popular *Applebee's Journal* in 1725 (signed 'Anti-Pope'):

> Writing, you know, Mr Applebee, is become a very considerable Branch of the English Commerce. [...] The Booksellers are the Master Manufacturers or Employers. The several Writers, Authors, Copyers, Sub-writers, and all other Operators with pen and ink are the workmen employed by the said Master Manufacturers (cited in Watt 1972, 53).

Marx repeats almost the same thing a century and a half later, in less ambiguous terms:

> |304| A writer is a productive labourer not in so far as he produces ideas, but in so far as he enriches the publisher who publishes his works (Marx 1969, 158).

It is only normal, in a social formation primarily defined by the Midas Plague, that any *thing* that satisfies a human want should also have a price tag on it. The difficulty arises when the entity that satisfies a want cannot readily be described as a 'thing'. How do we price listening to *Don Giovanni*? The answer seems easy: we price the opera ticket, or the vinyl record, or the CD it is printed on. Admittedly, none of these is the genuine article itself (the genuine article is an *experience,* something intangible), and cannot satisfy any want as such, except by proxy. How can we price the Theory of Evolution? We cannot, but we can price printed copies of *The Descent of Man* and *The Origin of Species*.

It is precisely at this point that the liberal/capitalist ideology intervenes and creates the profound confusion around so-called 'intellectual property'. Intellectuals and artists are by definition a peculiar bunch and have this strange

---

Facebook harvested data from its millions of users without consent and serviced it to advertisers and political actors through Cambridge Analytica, a private organisation also associated with the Russian involvement in the 2016 US Presidential Election. The same Facebook declares two years later, that they 'can remove or restrict access to your content, services or information if we determine that doing so is reasonably necessary to avoid or mitigate adverse legal or regulatory impacts to Facebook'(https://www.facebook.com/legal/terms/preview); thereby closing the barn door years after all the horses have escaped. In doing so they also demonstrate that the 'freedom to share', once it is monopolised under neoliberal rule, is nothing more than a sham and a lure in the service of the 'free' market, which does not allow anything but itself to be free.

insistence on being named the 'creator' (author, composer, writer, director, producer) of anything they produce. Mozart had probably wanted to be identified as the composer of *Don Giovanni*; Darwin has to be identified as the first person to conjure up the Theory of Evolution, and even I want to be identified as the author of this piece of writing. Riccardo Pozzo cites Kant in the matter of 'intellectual property':

> In *Of the Illegitimity of Pirate Publishing*, [Kant] considered the moral faculties related to intellectual property as an 'inalienable right (*ius personalissimum*) always *himself* to speak through anyone else, the right, that is, that no one may deliver the same speech to the public other than in his (the author's) name' (Pozzo 2006, 12)

To be sure, it was not always only intellectuals and artists who needed to 'sign' their works: guild masters and even journeymen did that too; as a matter of fact, until Fordism and Taylorism made it impossible to identify who did what, the 'ordinary' workers took pride in their work and identified with it as well. Unfortunately, contemporary capitalism made it almost impossible for most of us to identify with our work, except a few intellectuals and artists, but even then with a twist: Since these intellectuals and artists did not exist as a leisure class anymore, or under the patronage of noblemen or city-states, they had to 'earn their living'. They either did this by becoming affiliated with educational institutions (and thereby becoming wage-labourers), or by becoming petty commodity producers. And this is precisely where the very understandable intellectual request to be named as the 'creator' of a work and the need to earn money out of it became intermingled and confused.

Works of art or the products of intellectual endeavour retain their uniqueness, even under 21st century capitalism, but since most of these have become 'mechanically reproducible' (to use the term coined by Walter Benjamin), they are also priceable. This dual character inherent in the 'intellectual commodity' was already diagnosed by Kant:

> [A] Book, regarded from *one* point of view, is an external product of mechanical art (*opus mechanicum*), that can be imitated by any one who may be in rightful possession of a Copy; and it is therefore his by a *Real Right*. But from *another* point of view, a Book is not merely an external Thing, but is a *Discourse* of the Publisher to the public, and he is only entitled to do this publicly under the Mandate of the Author (*præstatio operæ*); and this constitutes a *Personal Right*. The error underlying the impression referred to, therefore, arises from an interchange and confusion of these two kinds of Right in relation to Books (Kant 1887, 90).

And copying or 'pirating' this commodity by third parties for the purpose of financial gain, according to Kant, is the same as cheating the author and his agent, the publisher:

Consequently, such an unauthorised Publication is a wrong committed upon the authorised and only lawful Publisher, as it amounts to a pilfering of the Profits which the latter was entitled and able to draw from the use of his proper Right (*furtum usus*). Unauthorised Printing and Publication of Books is therefore forbidden—as an act Counterfeit and Piracy—on the ground of Right (Kant 1887, 90).

So far so good. What Kant had stated in the late 18th century holds true until the late 20th century, as far as 'mechanical reproduction' of works of art or other intellectual endeavour are concerned. From the standpoint of capitalist production, making a profit out of someone else's labour is rightfully considered theft, *unless*, of course, the one making the profit is the capitalist and that someone else is the labourer.

'The Age of Digital Reproduction'

The possibility of *digitally* copying works of art, and more generally, of intellectual endeavour, however, in what we may call the Age of Digital Reproduction with reference to Benjamin, radically changes things. Mechanical reproduction could only be done at a cost, each copy still costing something, raw materials and labour-power, therefore becoming in itself a thing of Value. Digital reproduction does away with even that, thus creating the commodity *par excellence* of capitalism, something the capitalist mode of production was looking for for ages: a commodity that can repeat itself indefinitely once an 'original' is produced, with no (or negligible) cost and effort whatsoever.[2] You write a book, your publisher places it on a server with internet access and sells it over and over again to a theoretically limitless number of consumers, just like it is happening now with hand-held book readers (like Kindle) and content providers (like amazon.com). Nothing is spent or worn out, no workers are paid wages. To be sure, there is the initial cost, but since infinite reproduction is now without any cost, the initial cost divided by infinity still asymptotically approaches zero. It is the proverbial eternal goose that lays golden eggs, forever.[3]

---

[2] This is not to say that 'material production' itself has become (or is in the process of becoming) a thing of the past. In global terms, everything still has a material cost; nothing is totally 'virtual': for a product to be infinitely reproducible, that is, infinitely downloadable, the end users have to have computers with internet access. These computers have to be produced somewhere, some parts in a labour-intensive line of production, making excessive exploitation of labour-power still an unavoidable necessity. These computers need to be powered, making the production and distribution of electricity another unavoidable precondition, and since energy production is still in the realm of scarcity, it becomes another important addition to the actual material Value of digital commodities. All these real costs, however, are not paid by the enterprises that distribute digital commodities, but by end-users themselves, either directly or through public governmental bodies, which is practically the same thing on a national level. The unit cost of the digital commodity for the capitalist enterprise that distributes it still approaches zero, while its material costs are paid by the end-users themselves, which actually doubles the exploitation inherent in digital reproduction.

[3] This development, by the way, once and for all does away with the capitalist 'Scarcity Theory of Value', hastily developed as an 'alternative' to the Marxist Labour Theory of Value, and since the early 20th century

Of course, this picture is too good to be true, for capitalism at least. Because at the same time, other people have the opportunity to copy it as well, and distribute it using the same mechanism, at which point the capitalist immediately starts to yell 'Theft! Highway robbery!' Žižek dates the moment when capitalism became aware of this fact back to 1976, much before the age of torrents, P2P networks, hand-held readers and other such devices:

> The crucial date in the history of cyberspace was February 3, 1976, the day when Bill Gates published his (in)famous 'Open Letter to Hobbyists', the assertion of private property in the software domain: 'As the majority of hobbyists must be aware, most of you steal your software. [...] Most directly, the thing you do is theft.' Bill Gates has built his entire empire and reputation on his extreme views about knowledge being treated as if it were tangible property. This was a decisive signal which triggered the battle for the "enclosure" of the common domain of software. (Žižek 2008, 422)

Since Gates' initial outcry, the internet has become a battleground between those who desperately try to keep the goose and the golden eggs under bolt and lock, and those who try to steal the eggs from under the goose.

We need, however, to make a distinction at this point, between those who try to sell the stolen golden eggs, and those who want to share them freely with others. In both cases, however, the drive to retain the private nature of intellectual property will remain the same: the capitalists do not care whether the people who ('illegally') digitally reproduce works of art and intellectual endeavour do it for a profit or not. And it is precisely here that we see another sore spot of the capitalist argument for intellectual private property: it wouldn't be hard to detect and stop people who post uncopyrighted material on their sites and charge money for them, since this cannot be done without a credit card transaction. You spot the sites that require credit card information in order to download, and if the material they are selling is not copyrighted, you prosecute them. But no, the capitalist system does not want to do this, because it would be 'interfering with the free-market', and hence damaging to the virtual marketplace they have ventured so hard to set up in the first place. And some people making a small profit out of uncopyrighted ('stolen') goods is not a serious threat to the system as a whole anyway, since a limited amount of swindling, fraud, thieving and conning is an unavoidable companion of capitalist economy, always semi-tolerated under controlled circumstances. What really *is* the big threat here, is the possibility that people may have found

---

taught as an integral part of any elementary course in economics, which claims that the source of all value is 'scarcity'. Once, however, a commodity becomes infinitely reproducible without any discernible cost, any talk about 'scarcity' becomes superfluous, to say the least, or, according to this 'Theory of Value', this commodity becomes 'Value-less', which makes the assignment of an exchange-value to it an utter absurdity. I owe this piece of argument to James Block, who voiced it during the presentation of the initial version of this essay in the 13th International Conference of the Utopian Studies Society at the Universitat Rovira i Virgili in Tarragona, Spain, on July 7th 2012.

a way to distribute and share things, ideas and products *outside the free-market,* in a way incomprehensible (and therefore dreadful) to capitalism. As a result, whenever you buy something digital (whether it is a book, a song, a movie or software), a considerable percentage of the price you pay is for 'security' that renders it 'uncopiable'. In fact, a considerable portion of *any* software that is sold on the market (both as actually written lines of programming and as cost) consists of 'security'. In other words, the software industry makes us pay for the so-called protection, but the protection is from nobody else but ourselves, since each one of us is considered a potential thief: we are already fined before we even start considering stealing!

Strangely (or, for a Marxist, understandably) enough, it is capitalism itself which created this impasse, inventing a system whereby the possibility to reproduce (some) commodities without cost reduces the Value (and therefore the exchange-value) of these commodities to practically zero. Once this possibility starts to actualise, capitalism turns back on itself and desperately tries to put the worms it has freed back into the can, but to no avail. This is precisely an instance of what Marx predicted in 1857:

> At a certain stage of their development, the material productive forces of society come in conflict with the existing relations of production, or — what is but a legal expression for the same thing — with the property relations within which they have been at work hitherto. From forms of development of the productive forces these relations turn into their fetters (Marx 1999, 2).

The digital reproducibility of information and eventually knowledge indeed leads to a huge advance, a leap in the development of productive forces, and it is the relations of production, the property relations, that both enable and hinder it. And, as we can observe from the emergence and instant popularity of radical ('pirate') parties all over Europe, this structural conflict definitely heralds a 'revolutionary situation': more and more people become aware of this situation and take action, sometimes only signing petitions, but sometimes involving in so-called 'terrorist' (hacking) attacks on capitalist and government institutions on the internet, while those who are supposed to be governing are less and less able to do so.

To be sure, it is not only 'books' that create this upheaval. Music and film industries are already hit hard, TV industry following close behind. Music industry almost resignedly tries to adapt to the situation, re-channelling its efforts to enhance the live experience rather than recordings, so free low-quality (MP3) recordings of almost every musical piece ever written become available, while musicians and producers concentrate on tours and concerts. Online, on the other hand, streaming platforms (like Spotify and iTunes) and a souped up YouTube (many features redesigned for a pay-to-watch version) try to compete with free-sharing by keeping the prices low. Film industry takes a similar path, although much more grudgingly and not without putting up a fight, of trying to make the live experience non-compatible with home-viewing of downloaded material, especially concentrating on 3D productions and visual effects that are meaningful only on the big screen.[4]

TV industry is another story altogether: it is impossible to turn to the 'live' experience in TV, since there is practically no difference to watch a TV show live or downloaded, except for a slight delay which becomes significant only for the news. But wait, one might say, aren't all these shows (except for cable and satellite TV) already free, using the 'air' for broadcasting, supposedly owned by the public? Yes, but with a slight difference: they also force-feed you tons of commercials between and during all shows, and the people who download and post these shows on the internet very inappropriately omit these commercials which are the life-blood of the industry. This is why TV industry does not (cannot) resignedly accept its fate like the music or film industries, and puts up a big fight, becoming one of the main sponsors behind the governments' authoritarian (and increasingly totalitarian) measures to 'protect intellectual property'. One significant outcome is the rapidly increasing number of streaming platforms (Netflix, Hulu, Amazon Prime, etc.), without commercials but with periodic fees, again, like the music industry, keeping the prices low in order to be able to compete with free-sharing.

The same problem with the force-fed commercials is a big issue in software as well: any 'app' you download for your mobile phone or tablet comes in two versions, one with commercials and the other without. For the commercial-free version, you have to pay, sometimes a lot, and if you don't, you have to suffer many poorly conceived and executed commercials which interfere with the function of your device most of the time. The app designers thus declare that watching the commercials is a chore as well as a bore, and freedom from them can be sold just like any intangible commodity, not only to us but also to the advertisers; and the advertisers also seem to be aware of this fact and reorganise their advertising options accordingly, hence the overall poor quality of the commercials on the internet.[5] Why do they suffer this unfavourable positioning? Because they are not at all concerned with the impact of their commercials themselves (which is the reason for the overall poor quality), but the personal data they harvest through them. The constant and all-permeating

---

[4] The reaction of music and film industries to the Covid-19 pandemic and the ensuing restrictions, however, remains to be seen. If the pandemic persists and large gatherings become less and less desirable for people, these industries may double back on their initial response and start demanding stricter measures against free sharing, which will support Agamben's prediction of a dystopian 'state of exception'.

[5] So, another myth bites the dust! For decades, the advertising sector force fed us the myth that advertising is itself a 'creative effort', akin to both visual arts and literature, and those of us who were driven to work in this industry (given the poor employment opportunities for the 'intellectuals'), shared this illusion to a certain degree, partly in order to justify their means of subsistence. Now the sector itself almost openly admits, by declaring its 'products' a chore and a bore, that it is nothing of the sort, its gilt already scraped off by the TV series *Mad Men* (AMC 2007-2015).

invasion of your privacy through these apps and the commercials contained in them is but another affirmation of the fact that capitalism as we know it has ceased to function in the internet era, and another, new-fangled capitalism which has substituted a millennia-old despotic trend for the fragile 'liberalism' that had persevered for its first four centuries, has taken its place. The *panopticon* of this new capitalism functions neither by the glass walls and ceilings of Zamyatin's *We*, nor by Orwell's obligatory two-way TV, but by handheld devices and computers you willingly buy, and by software you willingly download. If you are clever enough to see through this sham and scam, and start to use the immense technological potential offered by the internet for a freer community built on sharing and solidarity, however, the despotic/authoritarian face of the new regime will immediately clamp down on you.

The Resistance

The story of Richard O'Dwyer, a 24-year-old British student, is an exemplary case in this matter: O'Dwyer created a website, TVShack.net, which gave links to sites to watch TV and movies online. Although this act was at most a misdemeanour by UK laws, he was 'guilty' according to the US DMCA (Digital Millennium Copyright Act) of 1996, and punishable by up to ten years in prison. He, however, committed this 'crime' on UK soil and he was a British citizen, although the US authorities, wanting to make an example of him, requested extradition in 2012. Not surprisingly, the UK government (in the person of the then Home Secretary Theresa May), accepted the request almost instantly. O'Dwyer appealed, and while he was waiting for the outcome of his appeal, Jimmy Wales, the founder of Wikipedia, started a campaign to oppose the extradition, and although he paid lip service to copyright and 'intellectual property' in his petition, the rest was clear enough to demonstrate what he thought was at stake:

> Copyright is an important institution, serving a beneficial moral and economic purpose. But that does not mean that copyright can or should be unlimited. *It does not mean that we should abandon time-honoured moral and legal principles to allow endless encroachments on our civil liberties* in the interests of the moguls of Hollywood (.@ukhomeoffice: Stop the extradition of Richard O'Dwyer to the USA #SaveRichard - Sign the Petition!)

The campaign eventually succeeded and the US case against O'Dwyer was dropped. He was, however, fined a considerable amount of money under UK law.

Another and much more tragic instance was the case of Aaron Swartz, who was a programmer and long-time online activist for open access (see Swartz 2008): Swartz hacked into the JSTOR, using a guest account, and opened the academic journal articles stored there to free public use, which was, of course, unacceptable for the extremely profitable academic publishing industry. He was arrested, put on trial and eventually sentenced to $1 million in fines and 35 years in jail. Swartz committed suicide rather than going to jail, on January 11, 2013, at age 27. He was posthumously inducted into the Internet Hall of Fame, and, more than six years after his death, on November 9, 2019, his birthday was globally celebrated as 'Aaron Swartz Day'.

The phrase 'endless encroachments on our civil liberties' used in Wales' campaign, represents a return to the dystopian discourse of the late 19th/early 20th centuries, starting with H. G. Wells' *When the Sleeper Wakes*. The antagonist here, however, is not uncontrolled technological development, but rather the capitalist class trying to subvert the possibilities created by this development in order to conform to its property relations. The SOPA (Stop Online Piracy Act) and the PIPA (Protect Real Online Threats to Economic Creativity and Theft of Intellectual Property Act) legislations of 2011 which the US House of Representatives failed to pass mostly due to widespread international public opposition, were endlessly revived and came back again and again, like zombies in a bad horror movie. The real intention of the US government (and it is reasonable to expect it will be joined by many more governments all over the 'civilised' world) cannot be merely stopping and punishing the perpetrators of uncopyrighted content: this would be a futile act anyway, since the hackers and 'pirates' are at least as clever and knowledgeable as the government employees trying to identify and stop them, always finding a backdoor when a door is closed, always finding a way around any and all walls built by them. This is why new legislation for copyright protection essentially targets (and will target more and more) the end-users themselves, making not only distributing but sharing itself a crime.

This is a properly dystopian future we are looking at, with our private lives under the threat of constant surveillance, maybe not exactly like Zamyatin's transparent walls in *We*, or like Orwell's two-way TV in *1984*, but through our computers and 'smart' phones, which are taking up an increasingly large portion of our private and public existences. It is ironic, but again understandable, that (neo)liberal bourgeoisie, the champions *par excellence* of 'privacy', are trying to put the last nail in the coffin of 'private life' as we know it, proving once again that what they understand from 'privacy' is nothing else than private *property*. Those who permanently censure the so-called 'totalitarian' regimes like Iran and China for their internet firewalls, are now trying to pave the ground for much worse measures, but since for them the ends justify the means, and protecting the sanctity of private property and the free-market are the only worthy ends, they have no qualms in doing so.

The bleak prospect of a dystopian future, however, is not only due to the capitalist dread of the possibility of 'sharing' outside free-market economy. There is also another and structural threat to the roots of capitalist economy inherent in the discussion around intellectual property: the software industry, the most recent and most rapidly developing sector of capitalist economy since late 20th century, is almost entirely structured around intellectual property, since any software once researched and developed is likely to be reproduced endlessly at no cost. The same thing is applicable, *mutatis mutandis*, to biogenetic industry, the future of the food production of the entire planet, since any genetic alteration, once researched and developed, can be likewise reproduced endlessly at no cost. Most of the new 'genetically altered' subspecies of grain, for instance, that give a much more abundant yield and promise to be an effective way to fight famine which still is a reality of our postmodern, 'globalised' world, are also rendered infertile by the companies who develop them, so that they cannot endlessly reproduce themselves, and that farmers keep buying them year after defer year. Without this final bit of genetic alteration (which is utterly unnecessary except from the point of view of 'profit'), however, they, too, are infinitely reproducible without cost.[6] These two sectors are the 'future' of capitalism as we know it, and they are in direct conflict with the relations of production that gave them birth. It is not only a few books, songs, films or TV shows that are at stake here, it is capitalism as a whole. As I have already mentioned, Žižek calls this unresolvable conflict of '[t]he inadequacy of *private property* for so-called 'intellectual property'" one of the 'Horsemen of the Apocalypse':

> The key antagonism of the new (digital) industries is thus: how to maintain the form of (private) property, within which the logic of profit can be maintained (see also the Napster problem, the free circulation of music)? And do the legal complications in biogenetics not point in the same direction? A key element of the new international trade agreements is the 'protection of intellectual property': whenever, in a merger, a big First World company takes over a Third World company, the first thing they do is close down the research department. Phenomena emerge here which push the notion of property towards extraordinary dialectical paradoxes: in India, the local communities suddenly discover that medical practices and materials they have been using for centuries are now owned by American companies, so they should be bought from the latter; with the biogenetic companies patenting genes, we are all discovering that parts of ourselves, our genetic components, are already copyrighted, owned by others... (Žižek 2008, 422)

Capitalism has finally created what it was looking for since its early days of

---

[6] The same mechanism that works for making 'security' an increasingly bigger portion of any digital product (especially software) we buy, is applicable to genetically altered grain as well. An absurd portion of the research and development in this area is wasted in making these infertile, which doesn't have to do anything with their nutritional value. We again pay for the cost of protecting multinational companies' profits from ourselves as the usual suspects. I owe this argument about the parallelism between software and biogenetic industries to my colleague Chris Stephenson, a computer scientist who is also concerned and extremely knowledgeable about biogenetics and food industry.

the 17th century, diminishing costs (asymptotically to zero) and maximising profits (asymptotically to infinity), but it cannot contain this development within the confines of the capitalist mode of production. This is why, in the foreseeable future, the entire ideological and political (super)structure of capitalism (in both its liberal and neoliberal incarnations) has to make room for an authoritarian discourse and political structure, to be rapidly metamorphosed into totalitarianism, utilising forms already prepared by the so-called 'communist' (Stalinist and Maoist), or modern Asiatic-despotic experiences of the 20th century.

On the other hand, any dystopian prospect is structurally conflicted, and includes its utopian counterpart as a kernel in the very terms it is built upon. This is probably why popular culture is so insistent to see a utopian future in the internet itself, while (at least partially) ignoring the imminent authoritarian prospect that comes along with it. It is not the internet itself, immensely however, that contains the actual utopian horizon, but rather the conflicted circumstances it gives rise to by simply being there. The possibility of universal free sharing (of books, songs, films, shows, games and eventually software) on the internet outside the rules and regulations of a free-market economy is the utopian horizon made possible by the digital age, but it almost instantly overflows the digital medium and creates other possibilities, e.g. in biogenetics, by making food infinitely reproducible and therefore universally shareable.

The actualisation of the utopian prospect made possible by digital reproduction first and foremost entails a political endeavour, resisting the authoritarian, and eventually totalitarian, measures proposed and taken by the existing governments and capitalist institutions. This endeavour may be assumed by the newly created radical ('pirate') political parties, or by older oppositional parties slowly becoming aware of the transformative possibilities brought forth by the digital age. A campaign led by more than ten thousand scholars against Elsevier,[7] a major publisher of academic articles, mostly in online journals who charge academic institutions obscene sums for subscription and individual users even more obscene sums for a single article, was sponsored by Wellcome Trust, who declared that they will, in the future, make open-access publication of academic work done under their sponsorship a condition.

In 2018, the University of California challenged Elsevier for open-access to publicly-funded scientific research. The negotiations between the UC and Elsevier continued into 2019, and were ended as of July 2019, without an agreement. Consequently, 'UC's direct access to 2019 Elsevier articles (and older articles in some journals) is now being discontinued,'[8] This will result in

---

[7] See http://thecostofknowledge.com/
[8] https://osc.universityofcalifornia.edu/open-access-at-uc/publisher-negotiations/uc-and-elsevier/

a considerable reduction in Elsevier profits, but at the same time will deny access to many academic articles for UC scholars and students, a clear case of lose-lose. Without a doubt, Elsevier can still survive *this* loss, in order to put through the message that academic publishing for profit is 'here to stay', but the demand for open-access is not limited to UC (or US universities) alone: 'After unsuccessful negotiations between a coalition of Norwegian organizations and the academic publisher Elsevier culminated in cancelled subscriptions earlier this year,' states Diana Kwon (Kwon 2019), 'the two have successfully established a new nationwide licensing agreement. The deal, which was announced yesterday (April 23 [2019]), is a pilot program that covers a period of two years, during which articles with corresponding authors from Norway will be published open access in most of Elsevier's journals.'[9] The agreement only concerns 'articles with corresponding authors from Norway', but it is a start anyway. Many EU countries are into similar negotiations with Elsevier and naturally with the other academic publishing conglomerates Taylor & Francis and Springer (as of December 2019), so far without the same success.

The limited success of the 'resistance' of academic institutions against academic publishing monopolies forced the latter to step back and reconsider. Consequently, they realised that they have some things to learn from the smaller 'predators', who prefer charging desperate academics rather than bigger and better-organised institutions such as libraries and universities. In the neoliberal academic world of dog-eat-dog and publish-or-perish, academics were willing to pay for the publication of their research, in order to advance (or merely survive) in this world. Since many academic institutions proved to be tougher nuts to crack, the bigger conglomerates also turned to the desperation of these scholars, and invented the concept of 'hybrid' publishing. Now you either pay them for your articles to be open-access, or you don't, in which case the academic institutions pay them for subscriptions, and private individuals about $30-50 per article, a by-product of (and, in turn, one of the reasons for) which is the almost wholesale isolation of the scientific community and a total inaccessibility of scientific knowledge for the general public.

This is how clever monopolies turn a lose-lose situation into a win-win one, although the majority of the people (meaning us) belong to neither winning side.

The Gift

There is, however, another and more imminently utopian action to be taken by each one of us: intellectuals who have hitherto been content with assuming either of the roles designed for them by capitalism, who either become

---

[9] https://www.the-scientist.com/news-opinion/elsevier-and-norway-agree-on-new-open-access-deal-65789

moderately-paid wage-labourers (academics) or petty commodity producers (writers), or in many cases both, may join in the radical criticism of so-called intellectual (private) property, not only theoretically this time, but also in practice. The intellectual-as-writer has always been suspicious of their circumstances as petty commodity producers (except for a few extreme cases books are not a dependable source of income), but has put up with this situation and assumed that the royalties they were paid in some way compensated for the intellectual labour they spent in writing. Now, however, they are expected to become active accomplices in a much greater scheme: their royalties are being used by the capitalist system as a part of the excuse to rationalise the increasingly authoritarian measures taken to protect intellectual property. Admittedly, it is a small part, but an integral part all the same.

Maybe it is time for intellectuals to assume the notoriously romantic, Cyranoesque gesture of '*Non, merci!*' It may seem conceited or even arrogant (as most romantic gestures *are*), but in this instance it seems properly placed: Cyrano's gesture was against the late-feudal patronage system; he was refusing to let his pen for hire to a patron. Today's intellectual gesture cannot but be against the patronage of the entire capitalist system, which throws them bits and pieces of so-called 'royalties' and expect their silence in return. It is a partially successful strategy too: even if it cannot secure the voluntary silence of complicity, the capitalist system at least manages to create a profound confusion among intellectuals (about the wish to be named as the 'creator' of a work *and* the need to earn money out of it), which leads to a kind of ambiguous silence.

A limited but brilliant analogue to 'art as gift' in the digital age, comes from a completely unrelated field, off-line by nature, from what is pejoratively and indiscriminately called 'graffiti', or, more properly, street art. Not the monumental murals of Diego Rivera, which were most of the time state sponsored anyway, but the mischievously brilliant art of Banksy, who resists persecution and attempts to buy off equally consistently.

Let us be honest: a vast majority of intellectuals cannot earn a living by merely writing anyway, and they are (usually) bright enough to know it. They are more concerned that with the denunciation of intellectual property, they will lose the privilege of intellectual identification with their work as well; they just can't get rid of the capitalist dictum that in order to rightly *own* something, you need to retain the right to *sell* it as well. As the prospect of a digital age has demonstrated over and over again, however, this is not the case: the real right of ownership is in *the gift*, in the right to give something freely away, to share. I can sell anything that does not really belong to me (capitalists do it all the time), but I can only make a gift of what is truly mine. Nuccio Ordine reminds us that 'knowledge' is such a gift, and, insofar as it is freely given, it will 'thrust […] into crisis the dominant paradigms of profit':

In these coming years we need to fight this utilitarian drift not only to save science, schools and universities, but also everything that we call culture. We shall have to resist the planned dissolution of teaching, scientific research, the classics and cultural assets. Sabotaging culture and education means sabotaging the future of humankind. Some years ago, I chanced to read some simple but very instructive words written on a sign in a library of manuscripts in a remote oasis in the Sahara: 'Knowledge is an asset that can be transmitted without becoming poor.' Only knowledge—by thrusting into crisis the dominant paradigms of profit—can be shared without impoverishment. In fact, on the contrary, it enriches those who transmit it as well as those who receive it. (Ordine 2017, 111-112)

In 1970, Abbie Hoffman, one of the celebrated leaders of the 'Yuppie' movement, the more political and radical wing of 1968 in the US, named his book *Steal This Book*. Since no publisher would agree to publish it (the book was 'too subversive'), he had to set up his own press, prophetically called *Pirate Editions*. The book sold more than a quarter of a million copies and actually 'made money'. Hoffman admitted to have been 'embarrassed' to be on the best-seller list, but in that pre-digital age, the only indication that people read your book was the number of copies sold. Since then, things have changed: if Hoffman were alive today, he would probably prefer to post it online open-access, and still publish a hard copy for promotion. The hard copy would still sell (people still prefer to have a tangible book in their hand, so to speak), but the press run would not be even a rough indication of how many people actually read it anymore. Paulo Coelho declared in 2012 that he preferred that people downloaded free digital copies of his books, because it did not actually interfere with sales much, and the more people read his work, the better. Trent Reznor (of Nine Inch Nails fame) invites people to 'steal his songs', since the arbitrary marketing strategies of recording companies are actually distancing his work from potential listeners.[10]

By denouncing our right to sell our books and articles, poems and novels, and claiming the right to making them a gift, we may turn the romantic gesture into a properly utopian one. It is only books, one might say, and who cares about them? Well, we should not forget that all this discussion about 'intellectual property' actually started with them. Books are a good starting point, even though by themselves, and from the capitalist point of view of profits, they do not amount to much. Each one of us who write for a living (not in the sense of making money but in order to make sense of our lives) may try to strike a new deal with our publishers in order to make our work open-

---

[10] 'Has the price come down? [crowd: no] Well you know what that means. Steal it. Steal away. Steal, steal and steal some more and give it to all your friends and keep on stealing. Because one way or another these mother f—ers will get it through their head that they're ripping people off and that's not right.' For the quote and a video of Reznor's address to his fans, see: http://www.wired.com/listening_post/2007/09/trent-reznor-te/

access, open for sharing with everyone. The publishers may not like this new deal, but they are fighting a losing battle already, and the more they fight, the more they run the risk of complicity with the authoritarian measures taken by the capitalist market, and it would be a safe assumption to say that this is a path many of them do not want to take anyway, at least ethically and ideologically.[11] Granted, we cannot suggest that all journals go open-access overnight, but they may post back-issues online as soon as a new issue is published (some journals are already doing that). We may impose a time limit on the copyright for books, after which they go free-access; and, more importantly, we may all insist that our contracts include a clause forgoing any prosecution for copyright infringement, *unless* such infringement is done for unjust profit. Or, better yet, we may try to become our own publishers and distribute our works on-line, free-access, through crowd-funding, using platforms such as Patreon.[12] If this proves to be too much for a solitary writer and researcher, we may take a shot at organising for this end, helping each other, practicing solidarity in real life rather than in theory.

Admittedly, this is not a recipe for utopia realised today, but it is a utopian gesture anyway, preparing the ethical and ideological background for the bigger fights ahead, so that we will have a clean conscience when we join in the struggle (both theoretically and in practice) against intellectual private property in software, medicine and biogenetics. A clean conscience may not be much, but people instinctively *know* when you don't have one.

---

[11] The publishers (at least most of them) are not the real adversary anymore (unlike Defoe suggested in 1725); except for a few big (and some transnational) corporations; most of them are only small (albeit still structurally capitalist) enterprises, not making any 'money' to speak of, in one sense trying to make gifts of *words* to people. They are, however, also caught in the deadly impasse between fulfilling the necessities of the capitalist market (cost minimisation and permanent expansion) and producing 'good' books; many of them still live in the Age of Mechanical Reproduction, not utilising the internet except for promotion, and not benefiting from the cost reduction opportunities of digital reproduction. Most of them, therefore, are potential allies rather than enemies, if a bit unwillingly at first (nobody likes change if left alone), but allies all the same.

[12] In Brecht's *Leben des Galilei*, Galileo tells Andrea Sarti that, '[e]ven a wool merchant, cannot be content with buying cheap and selling dearly; he must also be concerned that the trade in wool can go on unhindered. It seems to me that the way of science also requires particular bravery in this regard. Science trades in knowledge, which is acquired through doubt.' (Brecht 1963, 142) We too cannot be content with writing for an imagined audience and forgetting about what happens next. We must see to it that our work reaches people unhindered.

CHAPTER 3

THE END OF TRUTH AS WE KNOW IT

THE DISINTEGRATION OF THE UNIVERSITY DISCOURSE

'Those who feel "I possess Truth" –how many possessions would they not abandon in order to save this feeling! What would they not throw overboard to stay "on top"– which means, *above* the others who lack "the Truth"!'

Nietzsche, *Gay Science*: 13

'The possession of truth is the death of truth.'

Nuccio Ordine, *The Usefulness of the Useless*

How 'Truth' Disappeared

Everybody lies. This is the unwavering motto of Dr. Cal Lightman, the fictional eccentric behavioural scientist from *Lie to Me* (Fox, 2009-11). And of course he is right: Everybody lies. Politicians lie more than others, as is required by their profession; so do insurance salesmen and lawyers. Sociopaths and psychopaths lie all the time, and the psychopaths, being more clever, educated and manipulative than the former, make you believe their lies most of the time. It is no coincidence that more than a fifth of all CEOs, the captains of economy (21% to be exact, as compared to 1% in the general population), are diagnosed as psychopaths, and get away with it almost all the time.[1]

People did not start lying all at once these last few years, in this so-called era of 'Post-Truth'. They had been doing it for millennia, and as a matter of fact

---

[1] 'How,' one is bound to ask, 'do you know this?' There is a story behind this finding, which, I think, is closely connected to our present subject matter. The high incidence of psychopathy among the higher echelons of corporate structures proved to be extremely exciting for the mainstream news media, and the initial study by Nathan Brooks and Katarina Fritzon became the source of many news stories in 2016, as soon as it was published. The original publication was: Brooks, Nathan & Katarina Fritzon (2016). 'Psychopathic personality characteristics amongst high functioning populations'; in *Crime Psychology Review*, Volume 2, 2016, Issue 1. The article, however, was soon 'retracted' (in 2017), and is now inaccessible. 'Retraction' is a suspicious word and it brings to mind a degree of scepticism about the authenticity of the data and/or the ethical and methodological integrity of the research. We do not need to worry, however, because in the retraction statement by Bond University, to which both authors belonged (http://retractionwatch.com/2018/01/12/authors-withdraw-paper-psychopathic-traits-bosses/), the reason for the extraction was explained as an involuntary or accidental minor 'plagiarism' by one of the authors. In the same statement, a re-publication with minor amendments was promised, but it did not, to this day, happen. On the other hand, a book with a similar name and by the same authors (with the addition of one more) is published by Palgrave Macmillan in early 2020 (Fritzon, Katarina, Nathan Brooks & Simon Croom [2020]: *Corporate Psychopathy: Investigating Destructive Personalities in the Workplace*. Palgrave Macmillan), so we can 'fact-check' our data, which still seems to be valid.

had gotten quite good at it, although the neologism, 'Post-Truth' began to dominate our lives more or less in the last decade, and became the name of an era starting from 2016, more or less coinciding with the Trump presidency in the US. It can be defined as a euphemism that conceals the 'true' character of this period, as the *trivialisation or devaluation of Truth*, its marginalisation into insignificance. 'Truth' has always been a rare commodity, usually not easily exchangeable for money or other goods. It always had many different layers of meaning, which confused people all the more: it had a variety of denotations and it served (1) as the opposite of a lie or falsehood; (2) as the opposite of a fallacy, as an approximation of 'correctness'; and (3) as *aletheia,* the philosophical concept for being in accordance/consonance with reality, nature or the cosmos, arrived at as a result of study, research, experimentation, reason, invention, divine intervention, revelation, introspection, meditation, and finally, wisdom.

The question has always been; how do we tell a truth from a lie? How do we tell the truth from a fallacy? How do we tell 'Truth' from a systematic misinterpretation/misrepresentation of reality? Throughout history, human communities needed a wide variety of 'truth-checking' mechanisms, organisations and institutions, because, as Nietzsche states,

> We simply lack any organ for knowledge, for "truth": we "know" (or believe or imagine) just as much as may be *useful* in the interests of the human herd, the species; and even what is here called "utility" is ultimately also a mere belief, something imaginary, and perhaps precisely that most calamitous stupidity of which we shall perish some day. (Nietzsche, *Gay Science*: 354)

In order to distinguish a 'truth' from a lie, one can use torture (or 'Enhanced Interrogation Techniques', as the CIA so insists), a polygraph, sodium pentothal, or another lie (as the police is allowed to lie during interrogation in the US). In a lighter, but ostensibly more 'scientific' vein, it is possible to make use of 'behavioural markers', the inevitable 'tells' of liars, just like the fictional behavioural scientist Dr. Cal Lightman already mentioned above. It is also possible to arrive at the truth by 'fact-checking', comparing a statement to the 'known' facts, provided, of course, one is certain of their 'already known' facts. A safer way is to test the inner consistency of a statement, to see whether it is in contradiction with other statements within the same narrative. Every liar makes a mistake at some point, because there is no such thing as a perfect liar: your memory fails you at one point; you make errors of logic; even if you are the perfect psychopath, intelligent, knowledgeable and manipulative, you will eventually fall victim to your unconscious desire to get caught, to show off your perfect lie proudly as if it is a work of art, and give yourself away by showing off.

To distinguish a 'truth' from a falsity or a fallacy is a little more complicated: How do we verify the 'truth' of astrology? No person or institution has the means (or the time, or the sheer patience) to 'truth-check' every astrological prediction. So we resort to reason and ask ourselves whether there is a logical connection between what happens in the heavens and in our everyday lives. If we follow the commonsensical but logically fallacious dictum, *post hoc ergo propter hoc*, we may sometimes be erroneously led to thinking that there is one; reason, however, tells us that *sequence* is not the same thing as *causality*, and hence most astrological 'truths' are the results of logical *non sequiturs*.

Even then, most of us are not equipped with the scientific methodology and background information to pursue this line of reasoning that would eliminate most lies and fallacies; so we resort to the opinions of experts, specialists and authorities. Thus, we are confronted with probably one of the most complex questions of the entire history of knowledge, science and philosophy: who authorises the authorities (a variation on Terentius' *'sed quis custodiet ipsos custodes'*)? Who knows how to distinguish these experts who are supposed to 'know' (Lacan's *le-sujet-supposé-savoir*), from con-men, frauds, hoaxers? Throughout millennia, an entire edifice of experts, sages, scientists, scholars and 'learned people' (intellectuals, *intelligents*, the *'illuminati'*, the *ulema*—the enlightened ones) have organised institutions to authorise the authorities. In the West, this edifice was mainly the Church, until the University gradually replaced it, starting from late 17th century. In the East, it was a whole sub-class of 'enlightened ones' (called 'the *Ulema*' in Arabic), not organised into a Church (or any structured body of clergy) or a University as such, but as an integral part of the ruling class, which gave way to the University only during the long, strenuous and profoundly problematical process of so-called 'modernisation' in the 20th century.

Universities and similar educational institutions originally offered us a grip on Truth in most avenues of life, but did this at the cost of a hierarchical structuring of society. The coming about of the University Discourse (as a result/by-product of capitalism and liberalism) changed this and made 'Truth' negotiable. This was, however, only *prima facie*: those who negotiated the limits and extension of 'Truth' were only a small fraction of society, trained and cultivated experts who somehow (and allegedly) possessed *a priori* knowledge on how facts and information in general should be interpreted, processed and utilised in order to produce 'Truth'. The purchase on 'Truth' offered by universities and the professions that derived their authority from university education, was never too firm or justified in the first place: it was an elitist claim, most of the time arrogant, almost always too self-assured, and it was abused far too many times. Starting with the original universities, Bologna and Oxford in late 11th Century, and approaching its contemporary structure with the Royal Society in 1680, the concept of the university was always closely connected to a 'patron', no matter whether this patron was a king/queen, an aristocratic family or belonged to the upstart bourgeoisie, and the scholars organised within its structure were always the dependants of (members of) classes other than

71

themselves. This dependency, which is still in effect, if not aggrandised by the dominant neoliberal takeover today, made scholars subservient *clients*, but at the same time privileged vis-à-vis the rest of the society, which created a conflicted structure, profoundly complicating capitalist relations of production in the field of production of knowledge.

The Construction and Disintegration of the University Discourse

Ian Parker informs us that:

> In […] the discourse of the university, the agent speaks from the position of knowledge. […] This agent speaks from within knowledge and treats the other as *objet petit a²*, and this agent speaks as if there were fixed grounding points of truth as master signifiers, and he turns the one he addresses into someone who does not know what they speak about, producing a barred subject.[3] (Parker 2014, p. 62)

University Discourse, one of Lacan's 'Four Discourses', bestows *agency* on knowledge itself, not referring exclusively to the university as an institution,[4] but also to other positions that are defined by specialisation and expertise (such as medicine, technology or law), which derive their authority from the university in one way or another. We expect our physician (hopefully) to be a graduate of a medical school, and we wouldn't pay an attorney without a law degree. In the Post-Enlightenment world, University Discourse has become the primary source of authority on Truth. This does not, of course, mean that this discourse is infallible; quite to the contrary, it fails often enough: medical discourse is rarely free of the interests of big pharmaceutical companies; law has to go along with the legal system already in effect, implemented by those who are, were or had been in power, usually independent of the university discourse; architecture and urban planning are restricted and shaped by everyday politics, and of course by the interests of construction companies; and even social sciences and humanities often have to pay at least lip service to the mores and traditions (not to say beliefs and truisms) inherited from an older, pre-universitarian age. That is to say, as long as University Discourse submits to the Master's Discourse, it is allowed to have at least a partial claim on Truth and speak from the position of knowledge. Any Master situated within what

---

[2] In Lacan, *l'objet petit a* (the lower-case *a*) or the 'small other' is the unattainable object of desire, as opposed to the 'Big Other', the prohibiting father who stands between the agent and their object of desire. The *objet petit a* is also called the 'object cause of desire'

[3] 'The barred subject' [$] is the eternally split/prohibited subject due to its primal lack of having been forcefully separated from its mother, its primordial symbiote.

[4] 'Although Lacan's notion of "university discourse" circulates widely today,' says Žižek, 'it is seldom used in its precise meaning (designating a specific "discourse," social link). As a rule, it functions as a vague notion of some speech being part of the academic interpretive machinery. In contrast to this use, one should always bear in mind that, for Lacan, university discourse is not directly linked to the university as a social institution…' (Žižek; http://www.lacan.com/zizfour.htm)

we call civilisation, is also situated in a covenant of brothers, supposed peers sharing power, with a hard kernel of the primordial father, whom they have already symbolically killed, not able to emerge himself as an independent agent anymore, but adulterating every potential agent (Freud 2001, 164-165). In Lacan, the resultant profoundly conflicted network is called the Master's Discourse. This conflicted structure is the foundation on which the asymmetrical equilibrium between the material rulers, the owners of the means of production and of political power and brute force, and the leisure class (the intelligentsia, the enlightened, the *ulema*) who have the means and time to spend in the delicate process to produce, transmit and disseminate knowledge and construct what we call 'Truth'.[5] Since the Master's Discourse this leisure class submits to has nothing to do with knowledge or 'Truth' as such, however, it has to be conflicted from the very start, claiming to speak in the name of knowledge and having a hold on Truth, but at the same time having to justify its existence constantly in the gaze of the Master, who is empowered by ignorance:

> The discourse of the Master is thus always characterised by a kind of fundamental ignorance with regard to its conditions; it proceeds in an unconditional manner and requires to be obeyed on the sole authority of its enunciation: law must be obeyed because it is law and not because there are good reasons to obey it. In the discourse of the University, on the contrary, utterances always refer to some field of knowledge; they purport to be justified by proofs and arguments. (Salecl 1994, p. 163)

The 'truth' of the University Discourse, therefore, is not the Truth we seek (or pretend to be seeking) all our lives: it is defective, often only a half-truth, and sometimes (but admittedly only rarely) a glorified 'big lie' as conspiracy theorists are so eager to believe. It may be the worst approximation of truth, as Churchill had said about democracy, 'except for all those other forms that have been tried from time to time.' People have been criticizing the 'Truth' of the University Discourse from without and within the University (the institution) for decades, but had not been able to suggest a better alternative, until that discourse was undermined and gradually mutilated by different and much less subtle agencies altogether.

Even the temporary half-truths that the University Discourse provides us with, however, do not come without a price. Quite to the contrary, it has a lot

---

[5] The conflicted structure of this discourse is apparent in the fact that although it is the ruling discourse ('The ideas of the ruling class are in every epoch the ruling ideas'; Marx & Engels 1998, 67), arrived at as a consensus, as a temporary resolution in the endless flow of class struggle, it is also constantly threatened by the ghost of the primordial father, which existed in the mythical world *before* classes, but is still present within this consensus from the very start and provides it with its primal moving force, its life energy, its *libido*, so to speak. This ghost endlessly vies for exclusive possession of *jouissance* (for and against every member), in which case no ideas, no ideology, no legitimation, hence no communication, indeed no language other than the simple expletive '*Give!*' would be necessary or possible.

of strings attached to it from the very beginning, offering us only a *handle* on Truth in most avenues of life, but at the cost of a hierarchical structuring of society:

> The materialist doctrine concerning the changing of circumstances and upbringing forgets that circumstances are changed by men and that the educator must himself be educated. This doctrine must, therefore, divide society into two parts, one of which is superior to society. (Marx, Thesis III on Feuerbach)

What seems to be happening throughout the last decade, is the gradual invalidation of the University Discourse as the ultimate authority on Truth, and hence the disruption and gradual dissolution of the hierarchical 'Regime of Truth' (Foucault 1976).[6] What remains is not what Marx had hoped to be a more egalitarian regime in which 'the educator[s themselves are also] educated', but rather a 'Humpty Dumpty Regime':

> 'When *I* use a word,' Humpty Dumpty said, in rather a scornful tone, 'it means just what I choose it to mean—neither more nor less.' 'The question is,' said Alice, 'whether you *can* make words mean so many different things.' 'The question is,' said Humpty Dumpty, 'which is to be master—that's all.' (Carroll 1871)

What Humpty Dumpty is talking about here is apparently akin to what we will later call a 'Master Signifier', a signifier around which all language is organised and provides an anchor, a 'quilting point' for all other signifiers, 40 years before de Saussure and almost 70 years before Lacan.

Now all at once, it seems, virtually independent of (or disconnected from) the criticism of the concerned intelligentsia, the University Discourse is under attack on two separate, but in some way connected, fronts. These onslaughts are almost dismantling this discourse and its 'Truth' along with it, which leave the former critics flabbergasted and hurrying, albeit reluctantly, to its rescue, but to no avail:[7] University Discourse is failing and consequently we are being left with no hold on Truth.

---

[6] Foucault gives a more or less comprehensive definition of the '*Régime de la vérité*' in '*La fonction politique de l'intellectuel*':
  –   By 'truth' is meant a system of ordered procedures for the production, regulation, distribution and circulation of statements.
  –   'Truth' is linked by a circular relation to systems of power which produce it and sustain it, and to effects of power which it induces and which redirect it. A 'regime' of truth.
  –   This 'regime' is not merely ideological or superstructural; it has been a condition of the formation and development of capitalism. And it's the same regime which, subject to certain modifications, operates in the socialist countries (I leave open here the question of China, which I do not know sufficiently well). (Foucault 1977, 14)

[7] We should check, for instance, the recent argument of Bruno Latour, who had been an ardent critic of the claim on 'Truth' and scientificity in the modernist discourse, but felt obliged, in the face of the 'post-truth regime', to defend it, albeit conditionally. (Kofman 2018).

This development is bolstered by another attack, this time on the media, a blatantly open one in (mostly) the East, in Turkey, Russia, China and all over the Middle-East, and a more covert one in the West, especially observable in the offensive of ex-POTUS Trump on what he terms 'Fake Media'. This is why many theories about 'Post-Truth' abound in these last few years (also from within and without the University), trying to explain and understand what is going on, and having been able to make little progress so far.

The attacks on the University Discourse come from (1) the rapidly growing network of (seeming) universal availability of *information*, rather than *knowledge*, through the internet and, specifically, the so-called 'social media'; (2) the rising tide of so-called 'right-wing populism', which caters to the latent popular distrust of the University Discourse by declaring it 'elitist' and offering its own slipshod pseudo-truth (apparently based on, e.g., ex-POTUS Trump's Counsellor Kellyanne Conway's 'alternative facts') instead. We should, therefore, try to understand these two attacks, along with the one on media, in both its traditional and 'social media' incarnations, each in itself and in relation to the others.

The death of Truth becomes the fertile ground on which today's ultra-right populism may flourish. Wherever this ultra-right populism prevails, it first discredits and dismisses University Discourse as the haphazard blabber of the 'elite'. By a sleight of hand, it quickly replaces in the public imagination, the actual rulers/exploiters, who possess/control the real means of production and of brute force, with the intellectual/cultivated sub-class of society, counting on the structural, almost (but only *almost*) instinctual *ressentiment* of the masses towards this stratum, therefore depriving the public of the only reference point of Truth it ever had.

Neoliberalism Goes to College

'The Trivialisation of Truth' started a long time before the so-called era of Post-Truth, with (1) the 'Neoliberal Takeover of Higher Education' and (2) the (potentially) universal access to *information without knowledge* through the internet and in social media. These two instances resulted in the *ultimate dissociation of information from knowledge*, by making universities purveyors of practical and 'useful' (that is, useful for the capitalist establishment) information and gradually dismantling 'useless' knowledge production (that is, 'useless' from the point of view of capitalism) in the form of humanities, liberal arts and social sciences. (Flexner 1939; Ordine 2017). This development caused a hasty and mostly heedless turn towards social media as the source of 'Truth', which flourished without any checks and balances from the intellectual strata of society (which were being discredited as 'the elite' themselves, due to the rising wave of right-wing populism) disrupting the old hierarchy without replacing it with a viable alternative. The neoliberalisation of universities created a dog-eat-dog regime in teaching-learning, research and academic publishing. In this new regime, scholars relentlessly compete for grants and eventually succumb to the incessant demand to publish (no matter whether they have something significant to say or not) in order to improve (or even simply *keep*) their position as scholars. (Busch 2017). The result has been a rapidly growing walling-in, a profound isolation of the University Discourse, thereby giving even more credence to the populists' accusations of 'elitism'. The grants eventually established a strong corporate control over university research, and the 'big' (and increasingly profitable) business of so-called 'academic publishing' reinforced this control.

To tell the truth (insofar as it is still possible), University Discourse was never free of all these: blind submission to a mediaeval hierarchy, nepotism, plagiarism, conceit and elitism, and dependence on external financers (be they states or private patrons) were always a part of the university structure. This is why the neoliberal takeover, which is but a more systematic and organised form of all these together, took place without a serious resistance from within the university, except for a few solitary voices who took the submissive/utopian component inherent in the university seriously (which was also there all along), as a space where knowledge was freely produced and shared.

Where this neoliberal takeover failed, especially in some countries in the 'East' and in South America (the most recent example being Brazil), in cultures recently 'modernised' or in the process of 'modernisation', the establishment resorted to brute force and tended to destroy University Discourse altogether. It did this by first covertly, and eventually overtly, promoting ignorance and obedience, without any need for justification.[8] This has become the fertile ground on which today's ultra-right populism may flourish, as well as its unmediated result. Wherever this ultra-right populism prevails, it first discredits and dismisses University Discourse as the haphazard blabber of the 'elite'.

The gradual walling-in of the universities, and the growing inaccessibility of intellectual production within and around universities, in academic publications almost completely inaccessible for the 'populace', led people to search for the 'Truth' elsewhere, mainly in the social media and more generally throughout the internet, where there are no checks and balances, and a lie or a fallacy has the same semantic value as 'Truth'. Therefore, the final outcome in the West was almost the same as it was in the East: an almost total *decollement* of 'Truth' from everyday life (Busch).

---

[8] In 2016, the Vice-Rector of Istanbul Sabahattin Zaim University, Dr. Bülent Arı, declared on live TV that he 'trusted in the acumen of the ignorant and uneducated people rather than the cultivated class', and that he was 'exasperated about the rise in literacy.' He was eventually forced to resign his position as a result of public outburst at his words, only to be immediately appointed to the Supervisory Board of the Higher Education Council (https://birgun.net/haber/cahil-kesime-guveniyorum-diyen-profesor-yok-denetleme-kurulu-uyeligine-atandi-139491).

In the 'democratic' West, on the other hand, and especially in the US and the UK, where the existing 'Regime of Truth', loosely based on the University Discourse and its dissemination in the (both mainstream and alternative) media, is rapidly losing credibility and being replaced with a 'Humpty Dumpty' regime; words have come to mean whoever the Humpty Dumpty in power chooses them to mean. In these countries, universities were supposed to be 'free' in both research and teaching, although research funding was mostly left to big business and the career paths of scholars were determined by how many grants they get and how they fare in peer-reviewed academic journals almost entirely owned and regulated by big publishing monopolies. Although this system has hitherto managed to maintain at least a semblance of 'Truth', the veil is dropping fast, especially in view of the rapidly impending climate crisis, and the scientists and scholars who managed to survive within this system are being forced to 'put up or shut up', that is, turn into activists as well as scholars, or act as if no such crisis exists.

Academic or 'peer-reviewed' publishing throughout the last four decades, has started to act like St Peter at Pearly Gates, or, worse still, like *Deli Dumrul*.[9] As it stands now, the existing Academic Publishing 'industry' not only stops all kinds of 'maverick' or 'subversive' ideas even before they are born (most scholars permanently self-censor, because 'publishing' has become more important than writing), but also stops anything published to reach the public by making all scholarly writing (1) conform to 'scholarly' paradigmatic and syntagmatic standards not penetrable by non-scholars; and (2) obscenely expensive lest they are accessed by people non-affiliated to universities.

In the last decade or so, academic publishing became a battlefield between some universities and NGOs demanding open-access publishing, and many publishing monopolies determined to keep the goose laying golden eggs under bolt and lock. Starting from 2012 some universities took a stand against academic publishing monopolies in favour of open-access. These developments, although positive on the whole, did not fail to create despicable by-products, e.g., 'predatory' journals which supposedly provide open-access, but charge desperate scholars obscene sums of money just in order to publish their studies (Bell 2017). More recently, partly as a result of the pressure from universities demanding open-access, the 'top players' of the academic publishing sector also partly adopted the predatory strategy (under the label 'hybrid') and publishing in academic journals evolved from 'publish or perish' to 'pay or perish', sometimes both (Hyland 2015; Michael 2018).

---

[9] Deli Dumrul (Dumrul the Mad) is a character from one of the tales in the Turkish *Dede Korkut* saga (The *Book of Dede Korkut* 15th century AD, although the tale in oral culture may be as old as the 10th century). According to the tale, Dumrul 'builds a bridge over a dried-up river bed, to collect *haraç* (extortion, tax), both from the ones who cross the bridge (33 *akcha*), and the ones who don't (40 *akcha* plus a beating).' (Çavdar 2019, 41)

Once the absolute necessity of publishing as the indispensable prerequisite of academic advancement and survival is firmly established, academic journals, their editors and 'referees' (peers) obtain an unprecedented power over 'writers'. 'There were about 28,100 active scholarly peer-reviewed English-language journals in late 2014 (plus a further 6450 non-English-language journals), collectively publishing about 2.5 million articles a year' (The STM Report, March 2015).[10] In the publishing industry there were approximately 110.000 employees at that time, and even if we assume that all of these were editors (which would be unthinkable), an editor would have to read and evaluate and give feedback on 23 academic articles every year. To share this burden, editors delegate unpaid reviewers ('peers'), most of whom do this as a chore, most of them not exactly in their fields of expertise, and definitely a significant number of them just in order to exercise this uncontested and arbitrary 'power' over their peers, all of which make up an extremely fragile system that does not *work* (Bal 2018). Richard Smith had asked the crucial question 'Who is a peer?' back in 2006, and the answer he suggested was not very promising for scholars who were then being eventually dependent upon that system:

> But who is a peer? Somebody doing exactly the same kind of research (in which case he or she is probably a direct competitor)? Somebody in the same discipline? Somebody who is an expert on methodology? And what is review? Somebody saying 'The paper looks all right to me', which is sadly what peer review sometimes seems to be. Or somebody pouring all over the paper, asking for raw data, repeating analyses, checking all the references, and making detailed suggestions for improvement? Such a review is vanishingly rare. (Smith 2006, 178)

Assuming that all the standards are met, and the financial hurdles are cleared, though, this still does not mean that there is a significant exchange of information (let alone knowledge) among the scholarly community. Biswas and Kirchherr remarked in an article (in a non-academic journal, of course) in 2015, which was widely shared in the social media since, an indication that many academics were sincerely concerned about the issue, that:

> Even debates among scholars do not seem to function properly. Up to 1.5 million peer-reviewed articles are published annually. However, many are ignored even within scientific communities—82 per cent of articles published in humanities are not even cited once. No one ever refers to 32 per cent of the peer-reviewed articles in the social and 27 per cent in the natural sciences.

> If a paper is cited, this does not imply it has actually been read. According to one estimate, only 20 per cent of papers cited have actually been read.

---

[10] *The STM Report* March 2015; https://www.stm-assoc.org/2015_02_20_STM_Report_2015.pdf.

We estimate that an average paper in a peer-reviewed journal is read completely by no more than 10 people. Hence, impacts of most peer-reviewed publications even within the scientific community are minuscule. (Biswas & Kirchherr 2015)

The truth is, although the output of academic research constantly rises, it does not mean that the sharing of information and knowledge rises as well: quite to the contrary, the more academic articles are written and published, the less they are read. Furthermore, as Biswas and Kirchherr rightly comment, we do not have any data that having been mentioned or cited in other academic publications means that what we publish are actually read. To name the elephant in the room, a fact most academics know but are not very keen to mention publicly, is that many people who submit articles to journals are slyly careful to cite or mention articles by the editors, the editors' favourite authors, or potential reviewers of these journals, probably without reading these in full. It is, therefore, no coincidence that when the open-source website www.academia.edu, which was a free sharing place for published and unpublished scholarly writing alike, went 'premium' a few years ago, the only thing they charged money for was not *posting* an article, not *downloading* an article, but only *seeing* where you were mentioned and/or cited. Academics as a community may be mildly (or sometimes severely) narcissistic at times, but the fact that they are willing to pay for this service (they must be, otherwise this 'premium' practice would have ended a long time ago) cannot be ascribed to narcissism alone: maybe they need some desperate proof that they are not shouting, like Midas, into a dried-up well.

As a further indicator of the inherent fragility of the peer-review system and so-called 'academic publishing' in general, it is a good idea to study the two notorious, unethical, but in their own way, successful 'hoaxes' (Sokal 1995 and 'Grievance Studies' 2018).[11] These two much publicised 'affairs' which purported to 'prove' the futility and arrogance of inter- and trans-disciplinary fields of study such as Cultural Studies, Gender & Queer Studies or Postcolonial & Decolonial Studies, only proved (if not their own futility and arrogance) the fragility and uselessness of the peer-review system (and the existing regime of academic publishing) as a whole.

To conclude, the isolation of universities from the public, by letting more and more people in as students (in the US and UK cases, as clients permanently

---

[11] For the 'Grievance Studies Hoax' (2018) see, https://areomagazine.com/2018/10/02/academic-grievance-studies-and-the-corruption-of-scholarship/; https://chronicle.com/article/What-the-Grievance/244753; https://slate.com/technology/2018/10/grievance-studies-hoax-not-academic-scandal.html. For the much older Alan Sokal hoax (1995), there has been accumulated a lot of literature, not to mention the book Sokal himself wrote, with Jean Bricmont, *Fashionable Nonsense* (1998), in which he sets out to 'devastate' the entire armada of contemporary French philosophers, guided by the false but apparently extremely colossal sense of self-esteem he gathered from having very cleverly deceived the editors of *Social Text*. (See, The Editors of Lingua Franca 2000, Holquist, et. al. 1996).

indebted to their creditors), but letting less and less knowledge out by creating a vicious atmosphere of rivalry and competition within, and erecting 'Trump's Walls' of academic publishing around, brings about an almost total collapse of University Discourse. In its stead, 'Truth' becomes a product of an endless bargaining between different forms of media, some already directly controlled by despotic and corrupt governments, and others easily manipulated by the rising wave of right-wing populism. What we need today, as scholars both from countries with despotic/authoritarian regimes, where a ruthless persecution of the academia is at full-throttle, and from the supposedly more 'democratic' ones, where academics permanently fall prey to the dog-eat-dog regime generated by the neoliberal university structure and the Academic Publishing sector, to join forces to make some concrete and specific suggestions and on how to confront the crisis of neoliberalised universities and academic publishing together, and how new venues of both teaching-learning and academic publishing can be created.

Two Sides, Same Fence

Ursula K. Le Guin challenges us with two hypothetical situations in her essay 'Stalin in the Soul' (Le Guin 1993, 213-224): a novelist (call him Y) who lives in a totalitarian country, writes a magnificent Science Fiction novel, a dystopia which is also a metaphor for his country. The novel never gets to be published there, and he is eventually exiled; but his manuscript is smuggled out of the country, translated into many languages. It becomes a source of inspiration for many and is imitated many times by distinguished authors. It is not, however, published in his own country and in his own language, even decades after his death. Another novelist (call him X) who lives in a 'free' country has plans for a 'great' novel, a masterpiece. His friends and editors, however, warn him that it will not 'sell'. So he temporarily turns to popular fiction instead, postponing his 'great' novel; he writes sword and sorcery books (or soft porn, or romance), becomes famous in his own right. His books get to be filmed, and he also becomes a scriptwriter. So, years later, he is relatively rich and somewhat famous, but his 'great' novel is still not written. It never will be.

The irony of this essay is that, novelist Y is not a hypothetical person at all: he is Yevgeny Ivanovich Zamyatin, who wrote the canonical dystopia *My* (*We*) in 1920, was eventually banished from the Soviet Union by Stalin, and died in exile. His novel was not published in the USSR and in Russian, at least until 1990s, but it was there for the world to read, and in writing that novel Zamyatin almost singlehandedly (maybe along with H. G. Wells) invented modern dystopian fiction. Novelist X, however, is a true hypothetical, because he is just a stereotype: he is everywhere (especially in the capitalist Western 'democracies') as an unfinished, unrealised would-be writer. He is defeated without a fight, because he never really fought; he has only capitulated to what

Le Guin calls 'the censorship by the market'.

People who live in 'free' and 'democratic' countries mourn after Zamyatin and praise his bravery; they have even helped him to be translated and published abroad, he was able to emigrate to Paris, and died there in relative peace, albeit a lonely, unhappy man, not being able to write anymore. Nobody knows or cares about novelist X's, because although they were 'free', they never had the audacity to exercise their freedom. They succumbed to censorship by the market, and forfeited the option to be themselves. The problem with our neoliberal age is that the number of novelist X's now far exceed the number of novelist Y's, but no specialised organisations care for them or try to help them.

'*Scholar* Y's' from countries with 'authoritarian' or 'totalitarian' regimes, who have been threatened, censored, jailed and harassed by their own governments, have SAR, CARA or PAUSE, which help them flee their homelands, settle down in exile and carry on with their academic studies somehow. To be sure, those who manage to do this constitute a small minority; the majority cannot even flee, and suffer what has become a catchword in Turkey for the last decade, 'civil death'. Even then, they struggle to organise networks of solidarity among themselves, with or without outside help. But who will help '*scholar* X's' from supposedly 'democratic' countries? They are far more numerous, and they cannot even complain because they are allegedly 'free'. Scholar Y's cannot help them in their own capacity, because they cannot even care for themselves and subsist (let us not deceive ourselves by naming it something else) on charity. It is imperative, therefore, that we find a common ground and acknowledge that our liberties are threatened by the same agent, rigorous capitalist control over the production and dissemination of knowledge, albeit in different forms, be it despotic/authoritarian (mostly in Asia, the Middle-East, Africa and South America), or neoliberal/populist (mostly in the West).

It is, on the other hand, not even so clear-cut geographically: the neoliberal onslaught, the ruthless commodification of knowledge and marketisation of the university system, is very much prevalent in the East/South as well, just as the authoritarian measures against freedom of expression, research and teaching/ learning are becoming more and more widespread in the West/North. Scholars in the East/South do not only face overt persecution and brute force, but also the same pressure to trivialise and commodify their work; just as scholars from West/North are threatened not only by lack of job security and eventual loss of 'academic position' if they do not comply with the prevailing neoliberal structure, but also summary expulsion from the 'academic community' if they dare speak out against this system.

Despite the different forms, therefore, the threat is the same: as scholars, we have lost (or rapidly losing) our hold on Truth, which was (and hopefully still is) our only *raison d'être*. Admittedly, that hold was already open to serious criticism from within or without the university: it was based on an orthodox and inflexible definition of scientificity, making any serious and radical advancement and transformation in how we perceived truth extremely hard to accomplish, especially in social sciences and humanities. That was, however, all we had, and now that we lost (or are in the process of losing) it, only now we begin to comprehend its immense value. Alas, there is no going back: entropy always claims its pound of flesh, and the *status quo pro ante* can never be established again. We can, however, turn this loss into opportunity, and start to think about new *spaces* of knowledge, of its production and dissemination, new ways of sharing. We can begin by sharing our imminent problem, helping each other, working together, by acknowledging that for all its dissimilarities in appearance, be it open coercion by brute force or a more covert one, the censorship by the market and the neoliberal structure in general, the problem of scholars today is one and the same all over the globe: the impending death of Truth, not as an absolute certainty, but as an ever elusive goal to strive for. It is the disintegration of University Discourse in all its culpabilities and fallacies, and its replacement by the Master's Discourse, the acceptance and confirmation of universal ignorance, where blind, unquestioning obedience is paramount.

Although the problem is the same at its kernel, the ways to deal with it, to come to grips with these threats come in many different forms: they are not only different on either side of the 'East'/'West' divide, in the old and new-fangled 'authoritarian regimes' on the one hand, and 'democracies' and 'welfare states' on the other, but also in various countries and cultures. The problems before us in Turkey or Iran, Yemen or Syria, and India or Bangladesh are also different from each other. Likewise, the problems before the scholars in the US or UK and in Nordic countries or Germany are different from each other. The only common thing among them is that, the bigger problem they are all facing cannot be solved exclusively in one country or in a single cultural space: cancelling student debt in its entirety alone (as Bernie Sanders suggests)[12] will not solve it; abolishing the peer-review system alone (as Mieke Bal suggests) will not solve it; and even replacing Erdoğan or Modi or Bolsonaro alone (as many of us among their respective subjects suggest) will not solve it. The problems, as they appear differently in different countries and cultures, are the various material aspects of the same global phenomenon, i.e., the profound crisis of capitalism as represented in the present crisis of neoliberalism in its 'democratic' and authoritarian incarnations alike. The only shot at a real solution, therefore, is a broad-based collaboration involving scholars from many disciplines and across many cultures and countries, scholars and intellectuals from 'both sides of the fence', the 'victims' of both the 'democratic' neoliberal establishment and the violent attacks by the contemporary

---

[12] Bernie Sanders, a potential Democratic candidate in the 2020 Presidential Election in the US, promised to cancel the entire 'Student Debt' if he was elected, which reaches the unbelievable figure of *$1.6 trillion*.

authoritarianism and right-wing populism; not the former helping the latter, an act of *charity*, but both working together, an act of *solidarity*.

Is There a Life after Truth?

To put it in Blochean terms, we seem to be in a state of transition, where the old discourse and structure of higher education is *Not-Anymore (Nicht-Mehr)*, and a radically novel way of (re)organising the production and dissemination of knowledge is *Not-Yet (Noch-Nicht)*. As Latour had already admitted in 2004, and repeated in no uncertain terms in 2018, the radical critique of the established narratives on knowledge and Truth still relied on a common consensus on these concepts, on a firm infrastructure on which both the *critique* and the *critiqued* can safely rest:

> I myself have spent some time in the past trying to show '*the lack of scientific certainty*' inherent in the construction of facts. I too made it a 'primary issue.' But I did not exactly aim at fooling the public by obscuring the certainty of a closed argument—or did I? After all, I have been accused of just that sin. Still, I'd like to believe that, on the contrary, I intended to *emancipate* the public from prematurely naturalised objectified facts. (Latour 2004, 227)

And later in 2018 Ava Kofman quotes Latour taking a step further:

> I think we were so happy to develop all this critique because we were so *sure* of the authority of science […] And that the authority of science would be shared because there was a common world. (Kofman 2018)

In the same article, Kofman also quotes Donna Haraway cautioning against the hazards of turning around and going the opposite way: '[I]t's also an important moment not to go back to very conventional and very bad epistemologies about how scientific knowledge is put together and why and how it holds,' warns Haraway. 'We need to show the bankruptcy of this climate controversy without closing down the fact that science is a set of situated practices and not capital-S science.' (Kofman)

Now that this supposed 'certainty' and 'authority' have proven to be not as firm as it once seemed, now that 'climate-change-deniers', 'flat-earthers', 'intelligent-designers' and 'vaccine-deniers' enjoy almost the same credit (in the 'popular' media at least) as the respected scientists and scholars of old, and an ex-contractor politico invents his 'alternative facts' and makes half a country believe him, the critics of the old 'regime of truth' realise that *critique as such* is not (and has never been) sufficient. What we needed (and still need) was a utopian horizon[13] alongside the critique of all that exists, a Not-Yet-Conscious

---

[13] I must emphasise that this should be a utopian *horizon* rather than a definite, closed and duly narrated utopia, a utopian *locus*. For a discussion on the difference between utopian horizon and utopian locus, please see my *View from the Masthead* (Somay 2010).

(*Noch-Nicht-Bewußten*) to interact with and hopefully help shape the Not-Yet-Become (*Noch-Nicht-Gewordene*), a new way to imagine attaining, producing and disseminating knowledge:

> Thus the Not-Yet-Conscious in man belongs completely to the Not-Yet-Become, Not-Yet-Brought-Out, Manifested-Out in the world. Not-Yet-Conscious interacts and reciprocates with Not-Yet-Become, more specifically with what is approaching in history and in the world. And the examination of anticipatory consciousness must fundamentally serve to make comprehensible the actual reflections which now follow, in fact depictions of the wished-for, the anticipated better life, in psychological and material terms. From the anticipatory, therefore, knowledge is to be gained on the basis of an ontology of the Not-Yet. (Bloch 1996, 13)

Scientists, scholars, academics and intellectuals in general, who feel to be firmly rooted in the authority and certainty of the university discourse, are amazed at how flimsy that discourse proved to be, and how easily it collapsed under attacks from self-styled strongmen, PR 'experts' whose ignorance is surpassed only by their self-confidence, twitter trolls and cunningly manipulated 'fake news'. Some of them have even become unwitting co-conspirators in these attacks, as in the *ressentiment*-driven 'hoaxes' we have already seen (Sokal 1995 and 'Grievance Studies' 2018), and some (like Bruno Latour and Donna Haraway) were *accused to be* accomplices just because they had dared question the seemingly unshakeable certainty and authority of 'science' and scholarship. Both sides were culpable of either unquestioningly nestling in the comfort of the 'Truth' of this discourse, or criticising it without a reference to an 'ontology of the Not-Yet', or, what Foucault had named decades before the label 'Post-Truth' became the vogue and the crisis of the University Discourse as well as the University Establishment came to be well underway, a 'new politics of truth':

> The essential political problem for the intellectual is not that of criticising the ideological content to which science is linked, or to bring it about that his scientific practice should be accompanied by a correct ideology. But of knowing that it is possible to constitute a new politics of truth. The problem is not one of changing people's 'consciousness' or what's in their heads; but the political, economic, institutional regime of the production of truth. (Foucault 1977, 14)

Since 1977, however, the 'political, economic, institutional regime of the production of truth' has changed considerably, due, to a large extent, to the 'neoliberal takeover of higher education' (Busch), although not for the better. This 'takeover' did not only change the 'regime', but also the ways in which this regime connected to the world outside the main structures of the 'production of truth'. It created a new 'regime of truth' which is not exactly a structured narrative, but, as I have remarked before, a Humpty Dumpty regime, which is not sustainable and systematically destroys the 'common world' (Latour) which even the critics of the old 'regime' took for granted. The annihilation of this 'common world' is very much evident in the political, but at the same time economic and cultural schisms all around the globe: the elections in the UK (2019) and US (2020), the previous and current 'centres' of the modern world-system respectively, reveal to us two extremely divided countries, in which injustices in the distribution of wealth, knowledge and power are more explicit than ever. The authoritarian/autocratic dictatorships that pop up in the 'East' and in South America split each of the countries in these regions into two, and ethnic, gender and class alienation in each of them cannot be contained and concealed by the narratives of religion and/or the nation-state anymore. The University Discourse, which was supposed to give credibility and sustainability to the existing world-system is broken down by the same neoliberal onslaught aimed at consolidating it:

> In their efforts to bring the freedoms of the market world into being, neoliberals have through New Public Management, the Human Capital theory of education, and related changes imposed on everyone new forms of discipline based on various forms of hierarchical control. In contrast, [...] we need a world in which the civic, environmental, industrial, inspirational, opinion, domestic, and other orders of worth are not subordinate to the market order, but in which there is an ongoing discourse about promoting, (re)constructing, and (re)imagining multiple orders of worth. (Busch 2017, 116)

The present crisis (indeed collapse) in the University Discourse and corresponding structures of knowledge production and dissemination has once more demonstrated that: 1. Capitalist production is not compatible with the production of knowledge other than the knowledge useful only to capitalism itself (Raunig 2013); and 2. Capitalist forms of property are not compatible with so-called 'Intellectual Property' (Žižek 2008). Furthermore, it also brought to the fore the awareness (if only in hindsight) that contemporary forms of organisation and distribution of knowledge production, especially in our digital age, were already (that is, even before the neoliberal onslaught) incompatible with the hierarchic organisation of society, which is based on the ancient guild system. The UK system of Lecturer -> Reader -> Professor, or the US system of Assistant Professor -> Associate Professor -> Professor, and similar three-step systems in effect almost all over the world, are all based on the ancient Apprentice -> Journeyman -> Master system of the European Middle Ages, and almost as ossified and inflexible as this guild structure. Lawrence Busch proposes an alternative concept to replace 'hierarchy' in higher education, and connects this to the utopian imagination:

> [W]e would do well to pursue *heterarch[ies]*, [...] places where multiple orders of worth are discussed and debated, and where organizational goals are understood to be in flux in response to a rapidly changing organizational

environment. This is the case because new ideas, new means for enacting those ideas and citizens competent for life in a democracy, emerge from discourse and deliberation. [...] *They emerge from the design, debate, and implementation of imagined futures.* (Busch 2017, 117-118, my italics)

Once the mechanisms of producing ('Research'), transmitting ('Teaching') and disseminating ('Publishing') knowledge are reorganised 'heterarchically', that is, horizontally with multiple foci of 'power', and once the acquisition and transmission of knowledge are detached from the mechanisms of domination which are essential for career advancement and profit, we can start thinking about the uses of such knowledge for cleaning up the mess the obdurate profit-drive neoliberalism, as the most recent instalment of the capitalist world-system, left us with. It is only then we can (re)construct a 'Truth' that will be both the basis and and the product of the 'common world' we have taken for granted for centuries, and realised the value thereof once it was gone. This 'Truth', however, as Foucault has constantly reminded us, will not be free of 'systems of power', since 'truth is already itself power':

It's not a question of emancipating truth from every system of power – which would be a chimera, because truth is already itself power– but of detaching the power of truth from the forms of hegemony (social, economic, and cultural) within which it operates at the present time... (Foucault 1977, 14)

Although it is not possible, according to Foucault, to isolate truth from all connections involving and based on power, it is possible to free it from the various forms of domination and hierarchy, both the ones that are imposed on it by the recent reign of neoliberalism in knowledge production, transmission and dissemination, and the forms that precede it, steeped in mediaeval hierarchies and structures of domination. This emancipatory drive should come not only from within the university (or from what remains of it), but also from without, in the form of alternative loci of knowledge, of teaching-learning and research. The radical restructuring of the existing universities and the creation of alternative loci of knowledge can only be carried out by a co-operative effort from intellectuals and scholars that are being constantly hurt, victimised and excluded by the reigning neoliberal co-optation of universities and the anti-intellectual populist/authoritarian assaults all around the globe.

CHAPTER 4

THE GAME OF THRONES AS A FAILED ATTEMPT AT UNIVERSAL POPULISM

JON: How do you know? How do you know it'll be good?
DAENERYS: Because I know what is good. And so do you.
JON: I don't.
DAENERYS: You do. You do. You've always known.
JON: What about everyone else? All the other people who think they know what's good.
DAENERYS: They don't get to choose.
The *Game* of Thrones, Season 8, Episode 6

As it came to pass, the much celebrated/criticised but in any case, eagerly awaited 'grand finale' of The Game of Thrones TV series has been read as an 'in-depth' and extensive commentary on contemporary politics, complete with observations on populism, comparative government, democracy, feminism, multiculturalism and many more issues of our everyday lives, which accounts for the substantial popularity of the show.

It could indeed be read a commentary on all of these, but in the end, through the pompous albeit a bit rushed final episode, it boils down to an argument on the extensive effect of populism on our everyday lives: can a glorious leader, who is supposed to know beforehand what 'the people' needs, wants, is entitled to or deserves, achieve uncontested domination through conquest/violence and use their power in the interests of the people, eliminating all rivals who vie for such domination, branding them as elitists, self-serving tyrants, incompetent petty politicos and unworthy wannabes, but eradicating a considerable chunk of 'the people' as well in the process, not only as 'collateral damage', as is bound to happen in every violent revolution, but also as the target of his/her thirst for vengeance?

If we are to judge from the fan reaction in the social media, nobody was satisfied with this ending: most found it too rushed, many were frustrated by the tragic end of Daenerys, and nobody was very happy with the final political arrangement in Westeros. The two most popular protagonists, Jon Snow and Daenerys Targaryen did not end in the seat of power (the former went far North, the latter was dead), the symbolic seat of power (the Iron Throne) was itself destroyed in the process, and the 'Seven Kingdoms' evolved into one Empire plus a small Kingdom in the North. The 'Emperor' (although still addressed as 'the King') was almost the opposite of a popular/populist leader, symbolically and physically impotent (paralysed from the waist down and infertile), hence permanently changing the structure of succession, delegating it to an oligarchy. Many (if not most) fans would prefer a Khaleesi ascension to the throne, despite the fact that she unmercifully decimated most of the capital city's population although there was no resistance.

Very few really care about how 'the people' will carry on with their lives in the aftermath of the relentless struggle for political power (that took eight years even in real time) when the dust is finally settled, since *Game of Thrones* is a work of fantasy, and in (most) fantasy you don't really produce anything, other than heroic or villainous deeds, wisecracks or aphorisms, anyway.

People without Production

Most fantasy literature and cinema (and most SF, for that matter), is built on an utter denial of the fact that there is something called 'material production'. Because it is so boring, isn't it? It is something we are escaping from: the tedious routine of our everyday lives, the nine-to-five (and sometimes more) of ordinary capitalism, the uninteresting jobs we are forced into, but have to pretend we willingly chose, all these are why we seek refuge in the dreamland of fantasy in the first place, where no one produces anything other than adventure, wars and intrigue. There is one exception to this: weapons and armour have to be produced (so that there can be adventure and wars), so every once in a while, we visit a blacksmith (or the vast Orcish weapon shops in The Lord of the Rings).

There are of course other significant exceptions: David Eddings' Belgariad opens in a farm, where everybody labours in the fields or is engaged in some kind of productive activity, and the two main characters of the pentalogy, Garion and Polgara, are constantly working in the kitchen. Ged, the protagonist of the Earthsea series by Ursula K. Le Guin, was a goatherd in the Isle of Gont before he became a mage (and eventually the Archmage), and returns to Gont at the end of the third book, to become an ordinary working man, losing his power of magic, although still a protagonist (at least one of them) in the rest of the story.

In SF, things are a little different, but not much: in one of the earliest examples of the genre, The Time Machine by H. G. Wells, there is a huge underground compound of factories, run by disfigured and 'evil' Morlocks, as contrasted to the naïve, childish and pastoral Eloi who do not work at all, which disparity is the central metaphor of the story anyway. In one of the better examples of SF TV series, Battlestar Galactica, we observe starships entirely allocated to production, as contrasted to the exclusively military Galactica, but that is almost all.

Ordinary working people seem not to exist (or to matter) in Fantasy and SF.

Of course it is not much different in naturalistic (or mimetic) literature and cinema, but this is not our subject matter for the time being. Worse still, it is almost the same in narratives of history, and not only in the French sense either, histoire in French meaning both 'story' and 'history'. It is against this 'conception of history' that Brecht wrote his famous 1935 poem, 'Questions from a Worker Who Reads':

> Who built Thebes of the seven gates?
> In the books you will read the names of kings.
> Did the kings haul up the lumps of rock?

In the same poem, he also has something to say about the writers of Fantasy:

> Even in fabled Atlantis, the night that the ocean engulfed it,
> The drowning still cried out for their slaves.

The people exist only as passive subjects (or rather, a single, enormous and nebulous subject) in Fantasy: protagonists think and act in their name from time to time, make decisions, declare and win (or lose) wars, and the more they play the part of 'caring' for them, the more we like these selfless heroes. We pretend to 'escape' from the boring, dull reality of everyday to dreamlands, but we bring the most boring 'fact' along with us: that there are two kinds of people; the ones who speak, act and matter, the protagonists, and the ones who have to be spoken for, who need heroes to act in their name, and do not matter except as a shapeless mass without wills of their own as persons. These agents/heroes use the swords and drive the chariots they make, dwell in houses and palaces they build, and drink wine from the vineyards they labour in, but the people only make an appearance in their stories as some kind of a 'damsel in distress', somebody who need saving. Saving from whom? we are bound to ask. Well, from the antagonists of course, who are also agents/anti-heroes, the mirror reflections of the heroes.

To be perfectly fair, in the better examples of Fantasy and SF, the distinction between the hero and the antagonist is not that black-and-white; there are many 'shades of grey', and, in the best of them, even different colours, allowing for a more complex character development, Tolkien's protagonists (Frodo/Gollum, Gandalf/Saruman and even the short-lived Boromir) being the epitome of this. It is only in the later examples, however, especially in Le Guin, that the incontestable dualism between the protagonist/antagonist and the 'ordinary' people, as well as the fact that they exist almost entirely innocent of/apart from material production, is opened to critical inquiry, Starting from the third book of her *Earthsea* cycle, for instance, Le Guin returns her almost all-powerful hero, Ged, to his home island, to give up his magic power and live the life of an common person, working and producing as an ordinary artisan. In her later *Annals of the Western Shore* cycle (*Gifts, Voices* and *Powers*), the protagonists with magical 'gifts' live among the common people, and their 'gifts' are continually contrasted with their everyday existence.

It Ends with a Bang

As usual, very few people were interested in the fact that throughout eight seasons of the *Game of Thrones* (73 episodes in eight years), there was no indication of how the common people lived their daily lives, how they worked and what they produced, and under which circumstances. When we saw 'ordinary people', it was either as 'victims' of mass violence (e.g. Season 8, Episode 5), or its perpetrators (e.g. Cersei's 'Walk of Shame' in Season 5, Episode 10). The only 'production' scene we saw was (of course) the blacksmithing of the weapons that could kill the white walkers, the army of the dead, and the only 'main character' involved in it was Gendry Baratheon, who was very conveniently made a Lord later and inherited his father's title which was denied to him because he was a 'bastard'; thus he was forever liberated from such base and menial tasks. If we include 'intellectual production' (which we should), Samwell Tarly could be mentioned, who was a self-designated researcher, except that he was always the butt-end of a plethora of anti-intellectual jokes and intimidations all through the series, and an especially biting one in one of the final scenes (more on this later). Needless to say, he was also made a Lord and the Grandmaester in the end.

Immediately after the ultimate episode of the *Game of Thrones* was broadcast, many articles on the series were published, the overwhelming majority of which were critical of the last season and the ending. I will specifically focus on three of them, all presumably from a socialist/Marxist point of view, although none of them makes an effort to account for this lack of representation of the production process, and consequently its main agent, the labourers; they do not, however, fail to comment on its politics.[1]

Tüfekçi and Guy more or less agree on praising the first seven seasons of *The Game of Thrones* and criticising the last season as some kind of a deviation from this course. According to Tüfekçi, the first seven seasons represent a 'sociological' approach, telling the story from a 'sociological and institutional' point of view, in contrast to the 'psychological and individual' approach of the eighth. The argument itself is sound enough, except for the naming, the terminology: since my chosen field is Psychosocial Studies, I would strongly object to creating an artificial duality, sociological/psychological, as if these

---

[1] These articles are 'The Real Reason Fans Hate the Last Season of Game of Thrones' by Zeynep Tüfekçi (in Scientific American, https://blogs.scientificamerican.com/observations/the-real-reason-fans-hate-the-last-season-of-game-of-thrones/?redirect=1); 'Game of Thrones tapped into fears of revolution and political women – and left us no better off than before' by Slavoj Žižek (in The Independent, https://www.independent.co.uk/voices/game-thrones-season-8-finale-bran-daenerys-cersei-jon-snow-zizek-revolution-a8923371.html) and 'The hollowing out of Game of Thrones' by Simon Guy (in Socialist Review; http://socialistreview.org.uk/447/hollowing-out-game-thrones).

were terms for different and antagonistic world-views. In doing so, Tüfekçi (maybe involuntarily) accepts a popularised/populistic version of 'psychology', as branded by precisely the same establishment she criticises, and denigrates it, hoisting 'sociology' to a status akin to a Weltanschauung where it does not belong. The example she chooses is the story of Hitler:

> The overly personal mode of storytelling or analysis leaves us bereft of deeper comprehension of events and history. Understanding Hitler's personality alone will not tell us much about rise of fascism, for example. (Tüfekçi 2019)

Which is without a doubt correct, that is, as long as we accept the mainstream definition of 'psychology' as the endeavour to depict the personality traits or behavioural patterns of individuals isolated from the network of social and cultural relations they live in. There is, however, another 'psychology', e.g., the mass psychology of the Italian and German people between the two wars (as represented, for instance, in Reich's The Mass Psychology of Fascism), not to mention the many intersections between anthropology, Gender Studies, Postcolonial Studies, Marxism and psychoanalysis, and that brand of psychology indeed tells us a lot about the rise of fascism. Furthermore, no 'sociological' approach alone is sufficient to understand the function and transformation of institutions and masses, without taking into account this brand of 'psychology'. The supposedly self-evident split between sociology and psychology as forcibly isolated 'scientific' disciplines within the strictly compartmentalised 'scientific' discourse of today, makes both rather useless by themselves.

Having said this, I would of course concede the fact that there is an easily observable difference between the first seven seasons and the last, although I would rather interpret this divergence using Brechtian terms, as a shift from the epic to the (melo)dramatic. The Brechtian epic/dramatic distinction, however, should rather be seen as a scale rather than a mutually exclusive dualism: *The Game of Thrones* was not strictly an epic-dialectic narrative ever, and it did not exactly end up in pure melodrama, although there is a distinct shift from the former to the latter. This shift may not be as radical in content as Simon Guy seems to believe:

> The radical critique of class society and colonialism intrinsic to earlier seasons of Game of Thrones was replaced more recently with an individualised tale of psychology, characterised by a deep fear of its original revolutionary potential. (Guy 2019)

Having started reading the novels even before there was an idea of the TV show (and of course, having watched the show in its entirety), I would say assigning 'revolutionary potential' and 'radical critique of class society and colonialism' to it is a bit of an over-interpretation. Admittedly, it was radical enough to represent an at least pseudo-Brechtian Verfremdungseffekt in earlier seasons as contrasted to the last season, in which simplistic, quick and barely-explained fluctuations of behaviour and emotion observable in many main characters, intended to create a cheap emotional response, an easy catharsis in the audience, took over. George R.R. Martin, however, is hardly a Bertolt Brecht in his understanding and representation of class societies; he is rather a (fairly good) fantasy writer with a healthy rage against social injustice, pointless wars for domination and a grotesque lust for power, none of which makes one 'revolutionary' per se. But this is all we can expect from Martin: his political ideology fluctuates between the defence of a cursory democratic position and a yearning for a meritocratic order under the guidance of an enlightened despot. To be sure, Martin is not the sole 'proprietor' of the show. Although he is involved in every aspect of the production, HBO and the showrunners/writers (Weiss & Benioff) probably had the last word in 'wrapping up' the show in a hurry to make time for spinoffs, prequels and/or sequels, and convert the growing popularity of the show into quick cash. Coupled with Martin's already not-too-firm ideological hold over the huge epic cosmos he created, this undue haste practically 'ruined' the last season, at least for many fans.

Žižek's critique is more extensive, and in especially one respect, more 'ideologically loaded'. The reference to Stephen King, that the fans were annoyed not at this specific ending but at the fact that there was an ending at all, is a sound argument, revealing the open-ended quality of the universes created in fantasy literature and film. Of course this does not mean that any fantasy novel (or TV series) should not ever end, although some fantasy and SF writers seem to be attempting this impossible task: Robert Jordan's Wheel of Time series was an effort in this direction, going on for fourteen volumes, and only ended with the death of the author. It would rather mean that any ending or denouement should not also terminate the open-endedness of the universe, drain its options and reduce its possible paths and alternate courses of progress to one, that is, to the one which has just ended. What the final season of *The Game of Thrones* has done is mostly this in its haste to 'wrap it up' (except for some possibilities for sequels, which seem to be necessitated for business purposes rather than a respect for the open-endedness of the fantasy universe), and so the fans have every right to be annoyed, even if they cannot pinpoint precisely what it is that they are annoyed at.

With his critique of the Wagnerian renunciation of female lust for power, I would cautiously agree, maybe calling for a little more attention to the character of Arya, who never made a bid for political power, but nevertheless held more 'power' in her hands (at one point saving the entire world of the living), and at the same time successfully refusing to be used by any kind of political power, male or female alike. Unlike the other female protagonists, Arya has never been a nice girl bent on survival (Sansa), a ruthless Machiavellian (perhaps the most 'Wagnerian' of them all, Cersei), or a victim with a blind faith in her Birthright and 'destiny' (Daenerys). The female protagonist closest to Arya is Brienne of

Tarth, the supposedly 'masculinised' female knight. Arya, however, differentiates herself even from Brienne, since after they both have their first forays into sexuality in the final season, Brienne loses most of her 'power', helplessly crying after her 'man' but unable to do anything to assert her former commanding self, while Arya becomes even more powerful with the realisation of feminine sexuality. Her vigilante/feminine power superficially resembles Jessica Jones' in its 'darkness', but she is a better match for Buffy the Vampire Slayer, the girl who never uses her power to dominate others, always has her mentors and comrades alongside her, and in the end shares the power with everywoman who have a will to bear it.

Vox Populi, Vox Tyranni?

The final point in Žižek is the one I most severely disagree with: his characterisation of Daenerys as 'the only social agent in the series who really fought for something new, for a new world that would put an end to old injustices.' Although he puts a fine point on it by adding 'old' to 'injustices' with characteristic Žižekian subtle wit, intimating that he is aware of the fact that the Daeneryen 'new world' would have had its own share of injustices as well, it is apparent that he sees Daenerys Targaryen as some kind of a true revolutionary force to be reckoned with:

> And one cannot help but note that those faithful to Daenerys to the end are more diverse – her military commander is black – while the new rulers are clearly white Nordic. The radical queen who wanted more freedom for everyone irrespective of their social standing and race is eliminated, things are brought back to normal. (Žižek 2019)

We can concede that the claim that Daenerys 'wanted more freedom for everyone' is supported by the fact that she 'freed the slaves'. We should not, however, forget the fact that it was in another continent! In Westeros, where she sought her Birthright, that is, absolute power over the entire continent, there was no systemic slavery at all. The question becomes, therefore, what was her 'program', so to speak, to provide 'more freedom for everyone irrespective of their social standing and race'? And speaking of Westeros, it is important to remember that there were no 'races' there, everyone, including the hitherto excluded 'Northlings' belonged to the white race, except for the rather 'brownish' Southerners, which difference does not enter the text as a 'difference' at all. Admittedly, the fault belongs to George R.R. Martin rather than Daenerys, who imagined an all-white continent, limiting the black race to the 'other' continent of Essos. Daenerys 'freed' them, not because she was some kind of Moses of Martin Luther King Jr., but to transform the Unsullied, the former slave-soldiers, into mercenaries frantically loyal to herself (rather than the slave-owners).

We can understand what 'freedom' means for Daenerys in her very last words to Jon Snow.

> Jon: What about all the other people who think they know what's good?
> Daenerys: They don't get a choice.

So, Daenerys wants 'freedom' for people, only as long as she is the only one to 'know' what is good for them. What is 'freedom', one is bound to ask, if it is not thinking about or imagining what is 'good', or what constitutes a 'good life', and actively trying to accomplish it? The standard argument here would be that Daenerys did not mean 'people', but other Lords, Ladies, Maesters, would-be Kings and Queens: people who have the time and means to 'think' what is good for the people, but not the ordinary people themselves. They are too much concerned with everyday survival anyway; left to themselves, they would never go about 'thinking' or trying to 'know' what is 'good', until and unless another war comes about, when they would again be too much concerned with another kind of survival, simply staying alive and escaping the dragon-fire of their saviours. If in the end a new ruler provides them with a slightly better life and means, they should be thankful. 'Freedom', in this scheme, is strictly the business of the 'elite'.

We can, therefore, see that after a wide detour of fantasy (or should we call it traversée du fantasme?), we arrive exactly at the place where we started, at what everybody is talking about these days, populism. Let's 'render unto Caesar the things that are Caesar's', Žižek is not unaware of this: 'Daenerys [is] a new type of a strong leader, a kind of progressive bonapartist acting on behalf of the underprivileged.' (Žižek 2019) The argument here should be, of course, whether any Bonapartist can 'act […] on behalf of the underprivileged' or merely pretends doing so, but this is the subject matter of a much longer and much more detailed discussion.

The argument, however, that Daenerys Targaryen had intended to prohibit the involvement of the 'elite' in deciding what is 'good' for the people and thus 'setting them free', is the perfect populist one (doesn't matter whether 'right' or 'left', 'reactionary' or 'progressive') and it is not to be accepted lightly (or rejected in a hurry). The much-cherished leader of the Spanish 'Podemos', Pablo Iglesias, arguably a very good representative of 'left populism' for many political commentators, had already observed the relevance of *The Game of Thrones* to his movement in 2014, unfortunately for him, without knowing the end:[2]

> Daenerys manages to empower herself as a vulnerable woman in a world hostile to women. In order to do that, however, she must have the power

---

[2] It is significant to observe that on the cover of the book he edited on *The Game of Thrones, Ganar o morir: Lecciones políticas en Juego de Tronos* (2014), we see a picture of Iglesias himself seated on the Iron Throne. See Hans-Georg Betz, 'Populist mobilization across time and space', 197 in Hawkins et. al. (2014).

to conquer entire Westeros, the Seven Kingdoms, on the backs of her armies and her dragons, or else the peace she conquers for herself as a woman and for the slaves, will only be temporary: the weak need the power of the throne, public power, more than the strong, who already have their own private power for oppressing the weak and defend themselves against their likes. She knows that for any political (not merely moral) project, there is no legitimacy without power. (Iglesias 2014)

The actual ultimate episode, however, can only be read as an argument in the opposite direction. In order to conquer power and the legitimacy that comes along with it, Daenerys devastates the entire capital city, although its people do not offer any resistance, burning most of its inhabitants in dragon fire, proving once again that in order to gain power for and in the name of 'the people', one has to get rid of the 'people', not as a concept, but as a multitude of human beings. Furthermore, she does this in a way that leaves no room for the tired old argument that those who were killed were 'counterrevolutionaries' or those that opposed the change, or 'terrorists', or 'foreign agents'. She kills them, *simply because she can.*

This seemingly 'inhuman' act telescopes many past revolutions and their aftermaths into a single act, and hence could be rightly criticised as an oversimplification. We should think, however, of the French Revolution of 1789 and the Reign of Terror (officially 1793-1794, but actually 1792-1796) that followed it: what Daenerys did was to telescope the two events that were stretched over almost a decade, together in a matter of hours. In the Russian Revolution, the destruction extends over the entire Stalin Era, almost 30 years, starting from his grabbing power and legitimacy in late 1920s until his demise. Even the farcical figure of Louis Bonaparte grabs power in 1852, and after 18 years of comparative calm, he almost causes the destruction of Paris in a pointless war. Populism almost always destroys the people in the end, and Daenerys demonstrates this in a nutshell.

In 'rejecting' the populist argument, therefore, the last episode of *The Game of Thrones* quickly (in a matter of minutes) introduces a set of alternatives, ridicules and dismisses one of them (Samwell's call for 'representative democracy' in a feudal order), rejects a return to the status quo pro ante, and summarily decides on a kind of Magna Carta, where an oligarchy decides on who will be the supreme ruler in every generation, abandoning the concept of 'Birthright'. In doing so, it also dismisses the idea of an all-inclusive Empire (the North becomes an independent kingdom). Even this short argument among the 'elite' should make us realise the fact that 'Queen' Daenerys had not intended to be a Queen after all, but an Emperox (a non-gendered Emperor/Empress, to borrow a term from John Scalzi's *Interdependency* trilogy), because victorious (proto-)populism unerringly ends up in Empire, in its various incarnations of Caesarism, Bonapartism (of both Bonapartes, the first victorious and tragic in the end, and the second ridiculous but still tragic in the end), Stalinism and Nazism.

We can (and should) discuss the fortunes and misfortunes of populism at length, to our heart's content. Pro or con, the very fact that this discussion has become so central to our lives and theoretical endeavours, that we can see nothing but its validation or refutation in the 'ending' of a TV show, is proof enough that it is more than a purely theoretical or political matter. It has become something that touches most of us emotionally, and this emotion is nothing but fear: we fear disorder, we dread the chaos of revolution, rebellion or any kind of destructive transformation, and we are horrified of the directionless (or misdirected) violence of the masses. Accept it or not, we are also terrorised by the prospect of the planet which we have vandalised for centuries may finally hit back, and we cannot make amends without a massive, coordinated effort. We have all read about the Reign of Terror following the French Revolution, when everybody was happily guillotining each other in front of cheering masses. We have seen the Russian Revolution turning into a Stalinist dictatorship where even the victims were complicit in victimising themselves. We have seen many revolutions and 'wars of independence' in Asia, South America and Africa, ending up in worse dictatorships, massacres and some in open genocides. However radical our words may be, we all are terrorised, and some of us, even in a fantasy universe, have started (albeit under our breath) to pray for Lacan to be completely wrong, that there may be a 'Big Other' somewhere after all, an omniscient Philosopher King, a firm-handed but benevolent Glorified Father, an Enlightened Despot to listen to our counsel, somebody!

Žižek's sympathy for Daenerys and his portrayal of her as some kind of an Enlightened Despot, a revolutionary, is understandable in this sense, and it is completely in line with his recent (or maybe not so recent) turn towards a desperate acceptance (ironic maybe, but nevertheless acceptance) of some kind of meritocratic communism under a Benevolent Ruler. As for myself, I still have no hopes for (or excessive dread of) a Big Other. Whatever will happen, we will make it happen, not with/as the 'people' the populists promote and endorse, which does not exist anyway ('Le peuple n'existe pas'), but with/as a different people, not a presumed homogeneous unity, but divided and scattered, split and broken. Or, in other words, we should (re)start thinking and acting in terms of different and fundamentally conflicted entities presumably within 'the people', genders, races, sexual (and also various other) orientations, but most of all (horror of horrors!) classes. No 'Big Other', no meritocracy, no Benevolent Ruler, in short, no 'Populist' movement or leader (either from the left or from the right) can address the needs and wants of all these groups at the same time; it can only pretend to do so, and in so doing endorse and promote the regime of untruth that is already in effect.

In Monty Python and the Holy Grail (1975), one of the most ingenious spoofs of epic fantasy, there is a scene where King Arthur (portrayed by the late and much-lamented Graham Chapman) runs into a couple of peasants working by the roadside. In the dialogue that ensues, he cannot seem to convince them that he is indeed their ruler. The Old Woman (portrayed by the late and much-lamented Terry Jones) completely ignores him, convinced that they are living in some kind of an anarchist community. Dennis, the other peasant (Eric Idle), argues otherwise:

KING ARTHUR: [...] We are all Britons and I am your king.
OLD WOMAN: Oh! I didn't know we had a king. I thought we were an autonomous collective.
DENNIS: You're fooling yourself. We're living in a dictatorship, a self-perpetuating autocracy in which the working classes...
OLD WOMAN: There you are, bringing class into it again!
DENNIS: That's what it's all about. If only—

Arthur represents one of the most popular/beloved figures in English history everybody is nostalgic about: he is *almost* a democratic sovereign, an enlightened monarch, ruling by common consent, with a structured body of counsel (the Knights of the Round Table) and a renowned sage as his mentor (Merlin). Very few people think about how his reign concludes, in a devastating war with his own son (born of incest), in almost simultaneous filicide/patricide (the stories of Laius and Oedipus rolled into one), which leaves the entire land in ruins. In this respect, Monty Python have every right to ridicule this unconditional love of the English People for this monarch, which boils down to the desperate need for a Glorified Father, and Dennis (Idle) appropriately demystifies this by pointing out 'class', a concept almost always neglected in the search for a popular/populist leadership and enlightened meritocracy.

CHAPTER 5

THE PSYCHOPOLITICS OF THE ENTITLED VICTIM
THE COMING OF AGE OF CONTEMPORARY POPULISM

> The democrats concede that a privileged class confronts them, but they, along with all the rest of the nation, form the people. What they represent is the *people's rights*; what interests them is the *people's interests*. Accordingly, when a struggle is impending they do not need to examine the interests and positions of the different classes.
>
> Marx, The 18th Brumaire of Louis Bonaparte.

It is a good (and time-saving) idea for an(y) intelligible argument on populism, to start with a variation on the famous/notorious Lacanian dictum, *'Le [peuple] n'existe pas'*:[1] There is no such thing as ~~the~~ 'People', or, to make yet another variation (or inversion), this time of a much (indeed over-) used Latin phrase, *vox populi, vox inani* ('The voice of the people is the voice of emptiness'). The original phrase is '*Vox populi, vox dei*', 'the voice of the people is the voice of God', first used in a letter by Alcuin of York to Charlemagne in 798, but in a negative sense, in contrast to the 14th century affirmative usage by the Archbishop of Canterbury, or the much later use of the Whigs in the 18th century. The passage in the letter reads:

Nec audiendi qui solent dicere, Vox populi, vox Dei, quum

Tumultuositas vulgi semper insaniae proxima sit.

(Those who repeat that the voice of the people is the voice of God should be ignored, because the riotousness of the mob is always closer to insanity.)

Although it is possible to read Alcuin'of York's statement as a total repudiation of any mass movement (and in one sense it *is*), it is also possible to interpret it as a forecast (among many others) of, e.g., the events of January 6, 2021 in Washington DC, the already notorious 'Storming of the Capitol' by the Trumpist mob which devoutly believed all kinds of conspiracy theories cooked up by one of the most vicious proto-fascist manipulators in US history.

Indeed, you do not need to be a Lacanian to proclaim this. In the first (and only) session of the Russian Constituent Assembly in January 1918, Bolshevik deputy Ivan Skvortsov-Stepanov exclaims (in a speech that he claims to be pre-

---

[1] The original statement is the much-contested *'La femme n'existe pas'* [There is no such thing as ~~the woman~~], where Lacan argues against, not the actual existence of *women* or of *a single woman*, but the conceptualization of *the* woman (*la femme*) as an integral, undivided subject *as such*. As soon as *subjecthood* is attributed to *the woman* by language (which, according to Lacan, is structurally masculine), women are *subjectivised* (made *subject to* [masculine] domination) in the same stroke. Negating *this* 'subjecthood' is a liberating act, rather than a move to obliterate women.

approved by Lenin) that:

> How can you [...] appeal to such a concept as the will of the whole people? For a Marxist 'the people' is an inconceivable notion: the people does not act as a single unit. The people as a unit is a mere fiction, and this fiction is needed by the ruling classes.[2]

With the eventual rise of Stalinism in the USSR, however, this Marxist idea that "'the people" is an inconceivable notion,' was shelved forever. So much so that, even with the demise of the Stalinist brand of 'socialism', then with the demise of 'socialism' altogether, and finally with the rise of Putinism in post-Soviet Russia, the idea that the Father ('of nations', as Stalin was called) is the sole representative of 'the people' is still going strong.

In order to be able to represent something, something whose will is ethically, politically and socio-culturally incontestable, you first have to *invent* it. Only by doing so your own will also become incontestable. In order to attain absolute power, you must first create a 'subject' which incontrovertibly deserves this power, be very careful that this virtual subject does not exist in actuality (lest it may claim this power for itself), and then wait for the opportune moment when you can proclaim with pomp and fanfare that you represent it. Thankfully (for those who yearn for such power), such moments in history are not too rare to be underestimated.

Historicity of 'The People'

Let me start with a tentative attempt at definition and try to expand my argument from that preliminary hypothesis:

1. Populism is the coincidence [*Zusammenfallen*] and intersection of all ideologies built on the axiom that 'the People' is an actually existing agency in and of itself, as one of the poles of the dimorphism, 'the people/the elite' (Mudde & Rovira Kaltwasser 2017)[3]; and all political movements and self-styled 'leaders' that claim to represent (through elections, plebiscites, referenda or otherwise) such agency, without being a part of 'the corrupt establishment' themselves. (Hawkins, Rovira Kaltwasser & Andreadis 2018)[4]

---

[2] F.F. Raskolnikov, *Tales of Sub-Lieutenant Ilyin*: "The Tale of a Lost Day", 1918, first published in 1934, Moscow.

[3] 'Beyond the lack of scholarly agreement on the defining attributes of populism, agreement is general that all forms of populism include some kind of appeal to "the people" and a denunciation of "the elite." Accordingly, it is not overly contentious to state that populism always involves a critique of the establishment and an adulation of the common people. More concretely, we define populism as a thin-centered ideology that considers society to be ultimately separated into two homogeneous and antagonistic camps, "the pure people" versus "the corrupt elite," and which argues that politics should be an expression of the *volonté générale* (general will) of the people.' (Mudde & Rovira Kaltwasser 2017, 5)

[4] 'Rather than conceiving of populism as short-sighted economic policymaking (Dornbusch and Edwards 1991) or a combination of charismatic leadership, movement organization and mass appeals (Barr

2. Populism, therefore, *subjectivises* populations as 'the People' in both senses of the term: it makes them into *subjects*, supposed agents with a will of their own, and at the same time makes them *subject to,* and eventually *subjects of,* political entities vying for domination on the presumption that they represent them.

3. Lastly, since no universalised concept can be created in a vacuum, Populism has to invent an adversary, (other than the 'elite', the demarcation line between which and the Populists is always blurred and indefinite), internal or external, an antagonist against which the Populists can declare themselves protagonists. This adversary can be other nations, a neighbouring country or 'imperialism' in general, and their 'internal collaborators'. More significantly for *contemporary* Populism, it can be 'the immigrants', both as an external (e.g., Trump's 'Caravan') or an internal (e.g. many asylum-seekers, refugees and/or former *Gastarbeiter* in European countries) threat. The Populist insistence on xenophobia and anti-immigration policies arises from the fact that in order to give the impression to exist, the 'People' needs a social stratum *lower than itself,* another *subject* that is supposed to be *subject to* its will. Lyndon B. Johnson was reported to have said, 'I'll tell you what's at the bottom of it. If you can convince the lowest white man he's better than the best colored man, he won't notice you're picking his pocket. Hell, give him somebody to look down on, and he'll empty his pockets for you.'[5]

In order to be able to make my definition more comprehensive and comprehensible, however, I have to start at the root, by defining 'the People'. I commenced with the axiomatic assumption that the People *as such* did not exist, i.e., it is a discursive construct. It is made up of diverse social classes, genders and sexual orientations, races, cultures, etc., many of them not compatible with each other. Moreover, even leaving aside this synchronic incompatibility, the 'People' is also not the same thing throughout history, or even within the same historical period. Legal scholar David A. Strauss argues, in trying to demonstrate that the 'We, the People' of the US Constitution is just an illusion, not only synchronically, but also diachronically, that 'even assuming the text [of the Constitution] was the work of the people at some point, those people (leaving aside the most recent amendments) have not been around for a while.' (Strauss 2013, 1969)

This, however, was not always so; that is to say, my assumption is itself

2009; Weyland 2001), we follow others in defining it as a set of ideas – namely, 'a discourse that sees politics in Manichaean terms as a struggle between the people, which is the embodiment of democratic virtue; and a corrupt establishment' (Hawkins 2009; Mudde and Rovira Kaltwasser 2013). Populist ideas may be present to a lesser or greater extent in a policy or organization – it is not a dichotomous phenomenon – but it is the presence of these ideas that allows us to characterise something as (more or less) populist.' (Hawkins, Rovira Kaltwasser & Andreadis 2018, 2)

[5] Bill D. Moyers, The Washington Post, November 13, 1988.

historical and transitory: every discursive construct rests upon some kind of historical (or, depending on the context, biological), observable phenomena and advances by *deconxtualising*, that is, displacing and anachronising them. Insofar as the Classical Greek *demos* meant 'the people', for instance (which is not an exact translation, but we may let it pass for the moment), it *was* something tangible and definable at one point in history. It meant anybody who was not a slave, an artisan or a *metoikos* (foreign resident, immigrant) and of course, not a woman. So, even at the height of Athenian democracy, the *demos* consisted of only less than a fifth of the population.[6] Taken as a whole, we have a historically and sociologically definable entity in the *demos*, and it is safe to say that this *demos*, indeed, did exist, which means, of course, it was never identical with itself throughout history, even throughout the 'democratic moment' in Ancient Greek history. The same thing should be true, *mutatis mutandis,* with the Roman *populus* during the Roman Republic.

There is, however, no corresponding entity in the East during the same time frame: the mass of peasants and artisans, the subjects of the *Huangdi*, the Pharaoh, the Tsar or the Sultan did not constitute a 'People' in the Greek (*demos*) or Latin (*populus*) sense of the word: they were, rather, one pole of the binary *Avam* (the commons)/*Havass* (the elite) in Arabic. The so-called elite in this case still consisted of the subjects of the *Huangdi*, the Pharaoh, the Tsar or the Sultan, albeit in a privileged position: they were the soldiers (of rank and file), jurists or the bureaucracy, and although they were involved in actual decision- and law-making processes from time to time (mostly during *coups d'etat,* which were plenty), they did not have a firm and protected legal status in these processes.

The Greco-Roman 'Peoples' had slaves, immigrants and artisans *beneath* them; Eastern *Avam* did not, since there was no slavery *in production* in Eastern civilisations. This is why many European historians and philosophers mistook the peasants and indentured workers of Eastern civilisations for slaves for centuries.[7] Being the bottom echelon (and the overwhelming majority) of society, the Eastern *Avam* is much closer to the modern conception of 'the People', at least to the one consistently utilised by ideologues of 'populism'. They had the same legal status vis-à-vis the absolute ruler as the 'elite', the soldiers, administrators or jurists, although the latter had quite a bit more of

---

[6] We can safely assume that women made up a half of the population, and in the 4th Century BC, slave population was almost at par with the citizens (3-4 slaves per household). The estimated population of *metoikoi* were about 1:2 to citizens, and most of the artisans did not have political rights. So, even with a very conservative calculation, the citizens were only 20% of the population in Attica, probably much less.

[7] For a detailed argument on this, cf. my *Psychopolitics of the Oriental Father: Between Omnipotence and Emasculation,* 40-44. To be sure, Eastern Civilisations *did* have slaves, but these were not a part of the production process; they were only domestic slaves. Those who built the pyramids, for instance, were not slaves, as Western audiences were led to believe for centuries, but indentured workers, under contract for life. The difference may not seem important with regard to living conditions and such, but sociologically it is quite significant.

actual power in hand, and the *Avam* endeavoured to strike a balance by going over the top of the elite's head and unreservedly identifying with (and appealing to) the absolute ruler, or, in Karl Wittfogel's terms, the *Oriental Despot* (Wittfogel 1957). This created a constant state of *victimhood* in the East, an endless stream of petitioners, appellants, implorers and supplicants, 'victims' of wrongdoing mostly by the elite, who struggled to bring their cases directly to the absolute ruler, trying to bypass the bureaucracy with the help of a sizeable group of people who made a living by acting (or sometimes only pretending to act) as in-betweens and mediators. Even with the severely limited historical data on Asian Civilisations in his time, Marx clearly saw that the relationship between the Oriental Despot and his *kuls* (clients, bondsmen) was one of *representation*:

> Furthermore, the communality within the tribal body may tend to appear *either as a representation of its unity* through the head of the tribal kinship group, or as a relationship between the heads of families. Hence, either a more despotic or a more democratic form of the community. The communal conditions for real appropriation through labor, such as irrigation systems (very important among the Asian peoples), means of communication, etc., will then appear as the work of the higher unity—the despotic government which is poised above the lesser communities. (Marx 1964, 70-71, my italics)

When the term 'the People', which was put to deep sleep between the fall of the Roman Republic and the English 'Glorious Revolution' of 1688, was resuscitated, it was neither the Greek *demos* nor the Roman *populus* anymore, but rather 'the commons', much closer to the Eastern *Avam*, as is obvious even in the name of the political body that purported to represent it, the House of *Commons*. The actual term, however, taken over from the Latin root and made popular first by the US Constitution a century later ('We, the People...'), was closer again to the Latin *populus* than the British 'commons', since like that term, it was predicated over a yet lower echelon of society, the slaves (and, we should never forget, *the women*). In 1776, the slaves translocated from Africa (and survived the Atlantic crossing) made up about 20% of the population of the thirteen states whose 'People' proudly declared their independence from the British crown.

During the French Revolution, *Le tiers-état* was the seminal expression of the uprising, first made public in the pamphlet of the same name by Emmanuel Joseph Sieyès, denoting anybody who didn't belong to either the clergy or the aristocracy. *Tiers-état* came to be synonymous with *Le peuple* in Revolutionary France, and was imported to Britain as *The People* through Romantic apotheosis. The Germans resisted the Romanisation as usual and kept their *das Volk*. By late 19th century, entire Europe, with the exception of some die-hard communists and socialists who insisted on talking about social classes, had accepted the existence of this mysterious actor, 'the People', which nobody seemed to be able to define exactly. This difficulty in definition, according to Wallerstein, was largely due to the fact that bestowing 'peoplehood' on a group of people also meant to grant them certain political rights, which was not always convenient for the ruling classes:

> Of course, if we were ready simply to define the "people" as truly everyone, there would be no problem. But the "people" as a political concept is primarily used to refer to rights within a state, and thereupon it becomes contentious. What is obvious is that virtually no one was, or is, prepared to say that the "people" is everyone, that is, that truly everyone should have full political rights. There are some widely agreed-upon exclusions: not children, not the insane, not criminals, not foreign visitors — all these exceptions being considered more or less obvious to almost everyone. But then to add to this list other categories of exceptions —not migrants, not the propertyless, not the poor, not the ignorant, not women— seemed to many just as obvious, especially to those who were not themselves migrants, propertyless, poor, ignorant, or women. Who the "people" are constitutes to this day a continuing and major source of political controversy, everywhere. (Wallerstein 1999, 91-92)

A partial solution to this problem already existed in the language of the French Revolution: The Revolution did not only (re)invent the term *Le peuple* (e.g. Marat's *L'ami du peuple* [Friend of the People]), it also put into public use the appellation, *Citoyens!* 'Citizen', as a form of address, was the trademark of the Revolution, bypassing all honorifics and inherited titles, and equalising everybody vis-à-vis state and law, and, as such, was quite specific and definable. The same Marat who was extremely fond of using the universalising (and therefore confusing) term *Le peuple*, was not as ambiguous when defending the rights of specific groups of citizens (e.g., Protestants, Jews and Actors) to be elected to political assemblies.[8]

After two hundred and thirty years, the question 'Of what does the citizenry consist?' is still alive and well, even after various consensuses about former slaves, Jewish people, people of colour and diverse ethnicities, and, of course, women, have been reached: now we cannot agree upon the status of immigrants, upon the question 'Who is an immigrant?' or even upon the minute differences between immigrants, émigrés, refugees and asylum-seekers. It is not surprising, therefore, that the question of 'immigrants' would occupy centre-stage when trying to understand the phenomenon we call 'populism', especially its 'right-wing' brand.

In most of Europe 'the People' (*le peuple, das Volk, el pueblo, il poppolo*) was being used as a synonym of the entirety of citizenry by mid-19th century, and in a couple of decades, after the American Civil War, with the legal abolition of slavery, the American version came to mean the same thing. It didn't mean that

---

[8] Marat, Jean-Paul (1789). 'Jews, Executioners, and Actors', in *L'Ami du Peuple*, No. 77, December 25, 1789. https://www.marxists.org/history/france/revolution/marat/1789/jews.htm.

the controversy around citizenry was resolved; quite to the contrary, it would go on until women obtained full citizen's rights (Switzerland, 1971, although technically it was Lichtenstein, 1984), and although slavery was abolished in the US after the Civil War, African-Americans' right to an equal vote was constantly under threat until as late as 1964, when the 24th Amendment to the Constitution was passed.

It is no coincidence that the prevalence of the use of the term 'the People' in Europe and in the Americas coincides almost seamlessly with the use of the term 'the Nation', and its inevitable consequence, Nationalism.[9] 'The Nation' appears a bit later than 'the People' in North America, but not by much,[10] probably because it was slightly harder in the multi-ethnic, multi-cultural and multi-religious America to 'imagine' a nation. In any case however, when we entered the 19th century, we had three terms, 'the People', 'the Nation' and 'Citizenry', used almost interchangeably, throughout the 'Civilised World' (i.e. Europe and North America'), and by the end of that century, the rest of the world was *made* (sometimes forcibly) ready for the introduction of these concepts by the rapid advent and expansion of capitalism, usually disguised as 'modernisation'.

It would be wrong, however, to presume that as capitalism expanded, it one-sidedly imposed its portfolio of concepts without resistance and/or alteration onto lands not yet (or, left to themselves, would not probably be) 'modernised'. To the contrary, there was a lot of resistance, and although this resistance proved to be ultimately futile, there was an irresistible pressure for reaction and interaction, modifying, along with many structural and conceptual 'essentials' of capitalism, these three concepts as well. As a result, when, during the first half of the 20th century, a significant portion of the (rest of the) world was 'modernised' (i.e. became integrated into expanding system of capitalism), these concepts too were altered, modified and reimagined to fit the new reality of the 'modern' World-System[11] of diverse lands conjoining under a single mode of production but rooted in entirely different and sometimes intransigent social, economic and cultural (and also psychological and political) pasts.

For the purposes of the present article, the most significant 'acquisition'

---

[9] Since Benedict Anderson has done almost everything to depict and define the coming about and establishment of the concept of 'the Nation' as an 'Imagined Community' (Anderson 1983), I will not go into an extensive argument of this. Likewise, the concept of 'Nationalism' has also been extensively argued and 'dealt with' (the first references that come to my mind are Bhabha 2000, Chatterjee 1986, Özkırımlı 2000 and 2005), so I do not need to go into the discussion of how the concepts of 'the People', 'Citizen' and 'the Nation' are tightly interconnected.

[10] There is no mention of 'the Nation' in the 1776 Declaration of Independence; the term first appears in the 1789 Constitution, at the same time with the French Revolution. (Anderson 1983, 65)

[11] I use the term 'World-System' in the exact Wallersteinian sense, with the hyphen:
A world-economy is a large axial division of labor with multiple political centers and multiple cultures. In English, the hyphen is essential to indicate these concepts. 'World system' without a hyphen suggests that there has been only one world-system in the history of the world. (Wallerstein 2004, 99)

from Asiatic and African civilisations that is assimilated into the concept of 'the People' (and hence modified it to a significant degree), is the concept of Victimhood, and its transformation into a *Victim Identity* as a result of its encounter with capitalism.

Historicity of 'Populism'

Nadia Urbinati defines populism as

[...] a phenomenon that is parasitical on (because internal to) representative democracy, which is its true and radical target. This rivalry, I argue, does not necessarily produce more democratic politics, although this is populism's claim. As for its phenomenology, populism is a certain political style or set of rhetorical tropes and figures, yet is more than that because it seeks also state power to implement a political agenda whose main and recognizable character is hostility against liberalism and the principles of constitutional democracy, in particular minority rights, division of powers, and party pluralism. (Urbinati 2013, 137)

It is not surprising, therefore, to see populism (or something akin to it) emerging wherever and whenever some kind of representative democracy is in effect for some time. Accordingly, when we look at the *History of the Peloponnesian War* by Thucydides (Thucydides & Finley 1954), we find two proto-populist public figures (Pericles and Cleon) as early as the 5th century BC, at clashes with each other, both demagogues and public-pleasers, one an aristocrat and soldier-by-profession, the other a businessman-turned-statesman. According to Thucydides, a sworn enemy of Cleon and an ardent fan of Pericles, the former was a bully, a liar and a violent man who twisted every fact in his uncontrolled quest for power. American news media was quick to get hold of the obvious similarity between him and Trump and had moderate fun for a while.[12] The Cleon-Trump comparison is understandable (and yes, there is a definite similarity!), but it is also an anachronism, and like every anachronism, it may make us forgo our facts if we are overly insistent on it: we may, for instance, mistake Thucydides (a fan of Pericles) as an 'objective source' and overlook the fact that Pericles, although more soft-handed, was as much of a demagogue and bully himself, making him another proto-populist.

Athenian democracy at its height had these two 'parasites', who used the popular support they gain through demagoguery to play the various clusters of power within the ruling class one against the other, eventually achieving absolute power one after the other. From there, there is only one more step

---

[12] See, for instance: https://theconversation.com/can-we-learn-from-thucydides-writings-on-the-trump-of-ancient-athens-63391. https://www.politico.eu/article/thucydides-trump-why-the-white-house-is-reading-greek-history/. https://www.nytimes.com/2019/10/16/opinion/trump-history-lessons.html. https://www.spectator.co.uk/2016/04/meet-the-donald-trump-of-ancient-athens-he-won/.

towards (dreams of) empire, which inevitably leads to war and destruction: Pericles escapes this fate by falling victim to the plague at an earlier date. Cleon himself, a wannabe 'general' (*strategos*) with no military training, becomes the 'Commander-in-Chief' and is killed (along with his Spartan counterpart) in the battle of Amphipolis. Ironically, two centuries later Amphipolis will be the place Alexander of Macedonia will prepare his army for his Eastern conquests, this time for a real empire.

We can take, as another example, Marx's analysis of (both) Bonapartism(s). The quotation I used as an epithet from *The Eighteenth Brumaire of Louis Bonaparte* can be applied to proto-populists and populists throughout history and around the globe: substitute 'populists' for 'democrats' [*Die Demokraten*] and you will see that it remains perfectly valid. It is etymologically possible to go back to the Classical Greek root, δημοκράτες, and translate it to Latin, which then would become *populares*. From there it is a small step to *populists*. I of course do not pretend to claim that it was Marx's intention to critique the 'populists' in this passage written in 1852, when the term had not even been invented yet; but when read this way, the passage still makes perfect sense and actually contains the gist of my argument.[13]

When Fascism and Nazism were on the rise in Europe, there were a lot of discussions, especially among Marxists who were among the primary targets of these two movements, about the similarities between Fascism/Nazism, and Bonapartism and even Caesarism (e.g., Thalheimer 1930, Trotsky 1934). Although both writers were in agreement about certain similarities, they both warned of the dangers in making hasty identifications, lest we overlook the different class structures of the societies in which these phenomena occurred. Thalheimer particularly emphasised that Marx had warned in 1852, that so-called Caesarism and Bonapartism were fundamentally different as to their class connections, and although there is a similarity in the class *composition* of their respective supporters, the *classes* they helped flourish and capture and/or secure economic power were totally different. Thalheimer, especially, followed Marx in designating the rural and urban ('Paris') *lumpenproletariat* as the fundamental class component of Bonapartism (which was in fact not much different in so-called Caesarism),[14] and ascribed the political accomplishment of especially

---

[13] For purists, here is the original passage in German:

Die Demokraten geben zu, daß eine privilegierte Klasse ihnen gegenübersteht, aber sie mit der ganzen übrigen Umgebung der Nation bilden das Volk. Was sie vertreten ist das Volksrecht; was sie interessiert ist das Volksinteresse. Sie brauchen daher bei einem bevorstehenden Kampfe die Interessen und Stellungen der verschiedenen Klassen nicht zu prüfen. (Marx 1960, 144)

[14] Thalheimer quotes Marx to indicate that 'proletariat' meant two entirely different things in the Roman Republic and in 19th century Europe:

Lastly, I hope that my work will contribute toward eliminating the school-taught phrase now current, particularly in Germany, of so-called Caesarism. In this superficial historical analogy the main point is forgotten, namely, that in ancient Rome the class struggle took place only within a privileged minority, between the free rich and the free poor, while the great productive mass of the

Louis Bonaparte to his success in mobilising and controlling this sub-class. This sub-class of 'losers', so to speak in contemporary lingo, this 'underdog' of self-designated 'victims', found in both Bonapartes a voice justifying its existence, a champion to uphold its *ressentiment* of the so-called 'elite' of intellectuals and educated upper-middle class, although both, in the long run, served the interests of the actual ruling class, or, in Trotsky's terms, 'finance capital'.

I have to emphasise at this point that I am by no means ascribing trans-historicity to populism: it is a specific ideological/political experience, peculiar to the second half of the 20th century and onwards, and has very close structural and causal ties to neoliberalism (or the crisis thereof). Marx had argued against anachronising Bonapartism and categorising it under 'Caesarism'. Thalheimer and Trotsky did the same thing and tried to differentiate Fascism from Bonapartism, without ignoring certain structural similarities. The same thing should also apply here: contemporary populism is different from both Caesarism and Bonapartism, as well as from Fascism and Nazism. There is, however, a certain degree of connectedness between democracy and populism, as Urbinati rightly points out, the latter being a parasite on the former, and therefore we should be able to see emergent populism (or let us call it proto-populism for precision's sake) wherever representative democracy prevails (and eventually fails). A better explanation could be that (proto-)populism represents autocracy, the diametrical opposite of democracy, nesting as a hard kernel within it, emerging whenever it faces a crisis of expansion, therefore leading to empire (or at least attempts towards empire) eventually. This indicates a certain continuity from Periclean Athens, through Caesarism, Bonapartism, Fascism and Nazism to contemporary populism, a continuity afforded by the *lumpenproletariat*, this sub-class of 'entitled victims'.

Victim Identity vs. the Actuality of Victimhood

Contemporary populism has imported from the East the knowledge that the best way to suppress the actually existing agents that make up the people (individuals, social classes, genders, ethnicities, etc.), but keep the fiction that 'the People' as a unified entity is in itself an agent, is to make a *victim* of it: not actual victim*s* as individual entities, or as specific, definable groups (which most of the population already *are*), but as a unified whole, as an *identity*.[15]

---

population, the slaves, formed the purely passive pedestal for these combatants. People forget Sismondi's significant saying: The Roman proletariat lived at the expense of society, while modern society lives at the expense of the proletariat. (Marx 1975, 96)

In this passage, however, Marx himself seems to miss another historical analogy (not so superficial this time), between the ancient Roman 'free poor' who enjoyed a privileged position over the slaves and 'lived at the expense of society', and the 19th century (and indeed modern) *lumpenproletariat*.

[15] In this sense, as we deny the constituent *entities* and combine them in a universalised and nebulous *identity*, we also make them an *id-entity*, if one is allowed to engage in a little Lacanian word-play: it is more than a harmless word-play, though, as I will eventually try to demonstrate that this *id-entity* is closely connected

In order to make something perfectly clear from the outset: victimhood is *real*. It is real not only as a personal/individual experience, but also as the various existences of social or cultural groups, classes, ethnicities, localities, sexual orientations, ideologies, skin colours, languages or even as dialects, accents or brogues. From time to time victims, as any (or any combination) of these groups, seek not only individual justice for their injuries, but also a change in the judicial, cultural and social framework to ameliorate and improve their conditions. If this search becomes a permanent mode of existence, as it was in the so-called 'Orient', where every subject is a victim vis-à-vis a 'Primordial Father', unchecked by any organisational structure or rule of law, they may (and usually do) coagulate into *identities*, defining their being as one (or a combination) of these victim positions. Thus, they eventually become insensitive to the actual changes in their positions of victimhood, even when its conditions have been structurally altered or even do not exist anymore.

When the Eastern '*Avam*' becomes the model for the Western 'People', this borrowed definition of the concept of victimhood begins to possess the character of an *identity* rather than an actual experience, and in this sense, it becomes something *chosen*. The position and the identity of the victim, therefore, represent two structures that are fundamentally different: the victim *position* is the outcome of an event; it is something that *happens* to you, it is *real* regardless of your attitude towards it, so the victim in this sense is an *object*. The victim *identity*, on the other hand, is independent of the event: you *choose* to identify with it, to belong to it.[16] The victim identity, unlike the victim experience or position, *already exists before you become a victim* (or not), and makes it possible to identify with an imaginary victimhood, either merely *imagined*, or translated from the Real to the Imaginary. The victim in this case is a *subject*, in the Foucauldian sense,[17] whose subjectification is rooted in its self-victimisation. It is perfectly possible, therefore, if rare, to assume the identity of victimhood without ever becoming an actual victim. According to Jodi Dean, '[c]ommunicative capitalism's consumerism, personalization, and therapeutization create ideal discursive habitats for the thriving of the victim identity.' (Dean 2009, 7)

A victim identity, insofar as it leads to a demand for civil rights and a corresponding political struggle, is usually the inevitable outcome of a series of

---

to the *id-evil* (Žižek) that will arise from (or endorsed by) this self-victimisation.

[16] The best example for this is the situation of a 'closet gay': if a gay person (an orientation, not a choice), living in a patriarchal/homophobic culture (an accident of birth, not a choice), prefers to hide their identity (a choice), homosexuality for them is a position or an experience but not an *identity* as such. It is only with the *owning* of this position and the self-definition as 'gay' that *queer* becomes an *identity*, a starting point for political and civil struggle and/or for the establishment of a sub-culture.

[17] Foucault defines the two distinct meanings of 'subjecthood' as:

There are two meanings of the word subject: subject to someone else by control and dependence, and tied to his own identity by a conscience or self-knowledge. Both meanings suggest a form of power which subjugates and makes subject to. (Foucault 1983, 212)

prolonged victim experiences. The same experiences may often lead (depending on the political/social/cultural milieu) to coerced or voluntary ghettoization, to construction and consolidation of subcultures. The problem begins when the political/social/cultural environment gradually changes, and eventually tends to obviate these experiences. The victim identity, rightfully full of anger and resentment towards the system (and its supposed agents) that victimises it, sometimes overlooks this change, and insists on seeking revenge instead of justice, on blaming individuals and groups (often the wrong ones) instead of the system, and becomes self-righteous instead of rightful. Self-righteousness leads to an overpowering feeling of *entitlement*, and the victim identity coalesces into an *entitled victim identity*, an identity full of a *ressentiment*[18] no apology can soothe, no recompense can satisfy, no revenge can placate; an identity, in short, that demands only *jouissance*, something that is impossible to be given or received.

The contradictory situation of a social group that has long left the victim/subaltern position, but still trying to retain the victim identity, should make us suspect whether there is some kind of a perk, or, to use psychoanalytic terminology, a *secondary benefit* in this assumed 'victimhood'. In contemporary Turkish politics, for instance, the AKP (the Justice and Development Party currently in power) has insistently defined itself within the auspices of the victim identity from the moment it appeared on the political scene. It did so as the 'representative' of the conservative Muslim majority –as *the people, the nation*, or *the ummah*, depending on which term is appropriate for the specific moment and to the existing structure of alliances— victimised for decades by the laicist/Europeanised Kemalist elite. After seventeen years in power, after almost all state institutions are conquered and/or transformed, and the Kemalist cultural/political domination is either demolished or taken in tow, it still constantly renews its claim on victimhood every time there is a need for a state of exception, which means, in the present global crisis of capitalism and neoliberalism, almost all the time.[19]

So, the real question becomes, what is this secondary benefit of the victim

---

[18] I use *ressentiment* as described by Nietzsche:
Ressentiment itself, if it should appear in the noble man, consummates and exhausts itself in an immediate reaction, and therefore does not *poison*: on the other hand, it fails to appear at all on countless occasions on which it inevitably appears in the weak and impotent.
To be incapable of taking one's enemies, one's accidents, even one's misdeeds seriously for very long—that is the sign of strong, full natures in whom there is an excess of the power to form, to mold, to recuperate and to forget [...]' (Nietzsche 1989, *Genealogy of Morals*: 1/10)
[19] As the most recent example, after Donald Trump definitively lost the 2020 Presidential Election, he started a campaign of defamation against the election results, challenging them legally whenever possible (without any evidence whatsoever) and calling them a huge fraud. He went on gathering rallies (disregarding the pandemic circumstances), crying out 'We are the real victims here!' This last-ditch (and pretty pathetic) effort once more demonstrates that the victim identity is something a populist can never, ever give up, even when they hold the most powerful position in the world.

identity, that the individuals, social groups, strata, classes, or nations/nationalities, including those who have already abandoned that position and settled in the master/sovereign position, are so insistent on retaining it jealously? One of the answers I can suggest is this: because the victim identity (now we can read it as *id-entity*) gives us the opportunity to suspend our superego for a temporary period of time, providing a ready justification for all the evil we can do. Dean argues that,

> Accompanying the presumed weakness of the victim is a taste for cruelty. In the United States, claims for the rights of victims have stimulated increases in the brutality of the criminal justice system. [...] Neoliberalism's inevitable losses are displaced from systematic problems in need of collective solutions and concentrated onto the fantastic image of the individual criminal to be imprisoned, punished, tortured, and killed. (Dean 2009, 6-7)

The young Israeli soldier, for instance, who deliberately fires on Palestinian kids with the intent to kill or maim, must have 'turned off' or suspended his superego for a temporary period. The excuse for this 'turning off' is the atrocities against his ancestors during the Holocaust, which are real enough. It does not bother him, however, that there is no logical or structural continuity or identity between the perpetrators of the Holocaust and the Palestinian kids;[20] because the victim *identity* (unlike the victim *position*) deals in absolutes: he has been wronged (not he, himself as a person, but in his identity of *Jewishness*), and somebody must pay, no matter who. This is how any criticism of the Israeli government(s), political and/or public figures, policies and institutions, can be countered with the stock accusation of anti-Semitism, because any and all of these actual subjects are assimilated and absorbed within the imaginary universal of *Jewishness*: if you don't approve of the actions of Netanyahu, or the Likud Party, or the Gaza policy of the Israeli Government, why, you must be anti-Semitic, because all these actual agents are made identical with an imaginary Jewishness by a sleight of hand somewhere along the way.

The fact, for instance, that ex-POTUS Trump is an ardent supporter of the openly anti-Semitic alt-right white supremacists, does not cause him to be

---

[20] Even this absence of continuity is challenged by the narrative of victimhood whenever it becomes necessary, to the degree of (almost) absolving Hitler and the Nazis for the crimes of the Holocaust in order to incriminate the Palestinians retroactively. Israeli PM Netanyahu, for instance, declares in 2015 that, 'Hitler didn't want to exterminate the Jews at the time, he wanted to expel the Jew. And Haj Amin al-Husseini [the Mufti of Jerusalem] went to Hitler and said, "If you expel them, they'll all come here (to Palestine)." According to Netanyahu, Hitler then asked: "What should I do with them?" and the mufti replied: "Burn them."' (https://www.haaretz.com/israel-news/netanyahu-absolves-hitler-of-guilt-1.5411578) It is interesting to note, however, while distributing guilt between two (one actual and one alleged) 'villains', Netanyahu assumes the position of an omniscient/omnipresent/omnipotent ghost, eavesdropping a dialogue he does not care to document, while not letting go of the victim identity at the same time. He is both omnipotent *and* a victim, a fundamentally conflicted position that nevertheless defines the mode of existence of the present state of Israeli pan-Judaism and nationalism.

branded as anti-Semitic by the Israeli powers-that-be. When he supports the Israeli occupation of the West Bank, however, his critics are immediately labelled 'anti-Semitic', because in the populist imaginary there is no such thing as consistency: he can support the real enemies of 'Jewishness' all he likes, as long as he also supports the actions of the present Israeli state (not an actual victim anymore but an agent of domination donning the cloak of an imaginary victim identity), because the former is just a universal which cannot be harmed. What about the real acts of violence and hate against real Jewish people (tangible, flesh and blood individuals) committed by white supremacists, one is bound to ask. Well, they can always be blamed, using a simple sleight of hand and allowing for some passage of time in this era of short memory, on 'Radical Islam' or 'The Left'! In the UK, for instance, racists may engage in activities openly 'anti-Semitic', disseminate hatred about Jewish people, and cook up conspiracy theories with Jews as the chief perpetrators, for which they get a slap on the wrist. When the radical left within the Labour Party (including many Jewish activists) becomes a little vocal in support of Palestinian people, however, they become the 'purveyors of anti-Semitism' all of a sudden, and this accusation is used to isolate, suppress, and openly exclude them within the party.[21]

When we look at the situation from the perspective of actual victims of the present situation, however, we will see that the picture does not change much: the Palestinian suicide bombers had felt that they are not responsible for the civilians they hurt, because they had acted as a part of an acquired, embraced identity of the victim, rather than from an actual position. More recently, the suicide bombers of ISIS, and the white supremacist/racist attackers on mosques, immigrants and even their own citizens whom they believe to be empowering these immigrants also feel the same way, although they are not actual victims anymore, but only assuming a universalised victim identity.[22] Thus, their alibi is always ready: 'Since I am the victim, what I do should always be justified!' Here we observe a superego, no longer temporarily but permanently dismantled. Conscience becomes entirely ineffective towards the

---

[21] This, for instance, is from a letter sent to *The Guardian* by Jewish Feminist/Socialist activist, Lynne Segal, which the newspaper declined to publish:

Is the Labour Party hoping to solve its problem of antisemitism by getting rid of its Jewish activists? Are you laughing? I'm not. Every day I hear of another one leaving the Party in disgust at the misuse of accusations of antisemitism to further another agenda. [...]

We need to know what Labour's General Secretary is really up to in suspending Jewish members themselves for antisemitism, most recently Moshé Machover and Naomi Wimborne-Idrissi, who both happen to be well-known critics of the Israeli state in their work for peace and justice for Palestinians. Jews are being misrepresented as a community with a single view – and that is itself a form of egregious antisemitism. (Lynne Segal, personal correspondence)

[22] I will follow the example of New Zealand PM Jacinda Ardern and deprive these attackers of their names. The ISIS suicide bombers were usually nameless anyway (at least in the 'Western' media), and it would be a good idea to do the same for *all* suicide attackers, like the New Zealand attacker, and the Norway attacker/bomber in 2011, who has been 'named' much more than he deserved until now.

other, making its objectification absolute. Unfortunately, what has disappeared here is not merely the superego, but also the ego, the 'Reality Principle' whose primary purpose is self-preservation, since the act will end up in the disintegration of the self as well.

'The People' vs. 'The Scum of the Earth'

I have tried so far to ascertain that the 'people' that populists constantly talk about is merely an abstract notion, without a concrete, tangible will of its own. In the parlance of contemporary populism, however, there is a small minority within this 'people' which is most vocal and visible due to its enormous affective presence, its insatiable hatred for the 'elite' and its constant claim on victimhood, that the populists (usually intentionally) mistake for the entirety of the 'people', which is probably one of the most misinformed and dangerous metonymies of the last two centuries:

> The "dangerous class", [*lumpenproletariat*] the social scum [*Verfaulung*], that passively rotting mass thrown off by the lowest layers of the old society, may, here and there, be swept into the movement by a proletarian revolution; its conditions of life, however, prepare it far more for the part of a bribed tool of reactionary intrigue. (Marx & Engels 1969)

Ideologically and politically this 'dangerous class' never exactly belonged to the working class anyway, and therefore never had any real hopes for a classless, egalitarian and free society. Its ideology is driven by revanchism, vindictive not only towards the actual ruling classes who own/control the means of production, but also towards the intellectuals, the 'cultivated class' who possess (or has access to) a certain degree of societal and cultural power, and the middle classes who are financially (albeit slightly) better off; in short, towards all those who 'have' while they 'have not'.

The almost-instinctual opportunism and cynicism of the members of the *lumpenproletariat*, however, makes it possible for them to forget their hostility towards the actual ruling class, against which they are totally helpless anyway, and divert all their wrath, their destructive energy, towards more accessible and vulnerable targets, the intellectuals and middle classes, and even towards the actual working classes which have a more legitimate and stable position in society. They constantly feel victimised and that the world owes them, so anything they do (steal, cheat, rape, kill) is axiomatically justified.[23] They do not

---

[23] A very good example for this is the quite recent quasi-organisation of 'Incels' (Involuntary Celibates), mostly through the internet. The Incels describe themselves as a group of undesired males, victims of the existing 'sexual establishment', where good-looking and financially secure males and females 'find and mate with each other' while they are victimised and left out. So they find each other (almost all of them males) mostly on the internet and 'organise', develop a vindictive narrative of victimhood, and collectively fantasise (and sometimes actualise) acts of violence against 'entitled' men, and acts of rape and humiliation against women.

demand justice or equality, but only the same old regime with themselves as top dogs, with better cars, better homes, heaps of money and, unavoidably, beautiful women in great numbers (since the active elements in this class are predominantly male). This class is also particularly prone to manipulation, because, being cynical in the extreme, they believe that they are manipulating everyone else, all the time. So, any totalitarian leader worthy of his salt (Stalin being the epitome of such leaders) can manipulate this class, playing on their delusion of manipulating everyone, even occasionally pretending to be manipulated himself, like all good con-artists do.

The belief that the most exploited and most victimised section(s) of society will also be the most revolutionary, is simply untrue. There is no categorical causal relationship between being subversive or revolutionary, the will to transform, and being (or having been) exploited, persecuted, humiliated and ignored. All these latter can make you angry, spiteful, vengeful, or rebellious (also meek, submissive, sly and passive-aggressive), but not revolutionary. Being revolutionary entails not only being wrathful at the existing state of affairs, but also an ability to imagine an alternative, better future. For some time, you may believe that a combination or coalition between the wrath of the 'masses' (in actuality, the blind hatred of the most vocal minority within the masses, of the *lumpenproletariat*) and the wise, informed imagination of a 'leadership' will do the trick; but unfortunately, these two never 'mix'. Engels had foreseen this back in 1870, in his Preface to the second edition of *The Peasant War in Germany*:

> The *lumpenproletariat*, this scum of depraved elements from all classes, with headquarters in the big cities, is the worst of all the possible allies. This rabble is absolutely venal and absolutely brazen. If the French workers, in every revolution, inscribed on the houses: *Mort aux voleurs!* Death to thieves! and even shot some, they did so not out of reverence for property, but because they rightly considered it necessary above all to keep that gang at bay. Every leader of the workers who uses these scoundrels as guards or relies on them for support proves himself by this action alone a traitor to the movement. (Engels 2010, 98-9)

It is possible, of course, that a 'revolutionary leadership' can temporarily channel and manipulate this hatred, this 'explosive potential', and for a time make use of it during a revolutionary epoch, in a period of upheaval. When the revolutionary wave is slackened, however, they will see that they have been the ones that were used. Between 1792 and 1796, for instance, the Jacobins believed that they were using the furious, rebellious potential of the 'mob' to further the cause of the revolution, when they themselves were puppets in the vise of that mob's hatred. They ordered endless executions to satisfy that insatiable, vengeful desire, and eventually they themselves were also eliminated to make way for Napoleon Bonaparte. The problem with Jacobinism is not (only) that it is ethically unworthy of support, but (also) that it is doomed to fail, to make room for the shrewd totalitarian leader waiting in the wings, who can successfully manipulate the *lumpenproletariat,* and through them, the 'people'.

It is likewise erroneous to assume that the *lumpenproletariat* remained the same entity Marx and Engels were talking about in the 19th century. They exported their language, their expectations, their nebulous 'ideology', in short, their entire way of life to the *déclassé* petty bourgeoisie and peasants, to parts of the working class itself as they eventually gave up hope in a revolutionary change during the course of the 20th century, and even to the bourgeoisie itself, as it forcefully emerged in the 'modernising' parts of the world, without a history, a culture or a way of life of its own (Gunder Frank, 1972). Engels foresaw this too, and pointed out the 'transhistorical' aspect of the *lumpenproletariat* as early as 1850:

> The plebeian opposition consisted of ruined members of the middle-class and that mass of the city population which possessed no citizenship rights: the journeymen, the day labourers, and the numerous beginnings of the lumpenproletariat which can be found even in the lowest stages of development of city life. *This low-grade proletariat is, generally speaking, a phenomenon which, in a more or less developed form, can be found in all the phases of society hitherto observed.* (Engels 2010, 207, my italics)

The 'plebeian opposition' he mentions is also frighteningly similar to the so-called 'core' supporters of the present-day Trumpists, Bolsonarists, Erdoğanists, although in slightly better financial circumstances, since they have, by now, learned how to collaborate with the ruling classes and make considerable profits thereof.

The uncontrolled rage of these self-designated 'victims' which they do not fully comprehend themselves, turns them into a loaded weapon which may be dangerous for its wielders as well. Their fundamental disposition towards readily allying with the ruling classes is true not only on the societal, but also on the individual level. They have, for instance, no problem with male domination, but they cannot understand why supermodels and actresses they continually see on the media and imagine that they 'desire', are not theirs! So they issue themselves a license to rape. They want fast, expensive cars, and are so angry they do not have them, that they happily scratch the modest cars of middle-class people parked on the roadside; but as parking attendants and valets in super-expensive entertainment venues, they are willing to defend the expensive cars of the patrons with their lives in return for a chance to drive them for a couple of minutes to and from the parking lots. They have no objection to injustice; they just want the injustice to be in their favour. They don't question the magical power of money; they just don't like the fact that they don't have it, so they steal it. They see no harm in harassing Bohemian-looking people, long-haired, pierced and tattooed middle-class youth and girls wearing mini-skirts, because they don't look like them, but as bouncers at the doors of luxury nightclubs where much more exaggerated 'other-bodies' frequent, they eagerly serve to protect them. When they gang up to attack 'others', these gangs can often be guided or even coordinated by the state or 'the deep state', controlled and kept ready for the time when a versatile (meaning, not bothered by legalities) paramilitary force may be needed.

On the other hand, however, when they occasionally find a home in a 'leftist' or 'revolutionary' group, as pretend 'victims', their contagious *id-evil*[24] rapidly decays these 'leftist' or 'revolutionary' structures, especially in the last three decades when the basic ideological assumptions of 'the left' are daily challenged by the 'fall' of the 'Socialist System'. Their allure for the 'left' is, according to Dean, twofold, offering it both the permanent justification and the political irresponsibility of pretend victimhood:

> Shrinking the scope of political claims to those of victims needing recognition and redress also traps claimants in a double bind: to speak at all they have to demonstrate how they are harmed and vulnerable, how they are weak, inadequate, or suffering. They must speak as those who have lost, those who are losers. One who feels the political impulse to struggle, who is ready for a fight against injustice, is not injured enough to speak. For many leftists, the attraction of the position of the victim is thus double: one is always morally correct —for who can deny the suffering of the victim? — and never politically responsible —for victims are too weak and injured to govern. (Dean 2009, 5-6)

Once they successfully permeate a 'leftist' body, however, they rapidly give rise to violence as a goal in and for itself, and in a short while, they begin to target other 'leftists' and 'revolutionaries', instead of the ruling classes, and consequently this short-lived cooperation ends in various suicidal acts. The most fundamental problem with id-evil is that it must eventually destroy the 'self' that bears it. We shouldn't console ourselves, however, with the

---

[24] Slavoj Žižek describes 'id-evil' as,

[...] the evil structured and motivated by the most elementary imbalance in the relationship between the *Ich* and *jouissance*, by the tension between pleasure and the foreign body of jouissance at the very heart of it. Id-evil thus stages the most elementary short-circuit in the relationship of the subject to the primordially missing object-cause of his desire. What bothers us in the Other (the Jew, the Japanese, the African, the Turk, and so forth) is that he appears to entertain a privileged relationship to the object. The Other either possesses the object-treasure, having snatched it away from us (which is why we don't have it), or poses a threat to our possession of the object. (Žižek 1998, 99)

We can read Žižek's argument here (with reference to the issue at hand) as the insatiable thirst of the *lumpenproletariat* for the 'things', objects of desire that *other* classes have and it has not. Since it doesn't have them, they must have been 'snatched away' from it, so it has every right to try and get them back; it has a 'righteous anger' towards these classes whom it sees to have a 'privileged relationship to the object'. Since the ruling classes are not going to grant its desires at the drop of a hat, however, it directs its rage towards the other, easier classes, the middle-classes, the working-classes and the intellectual strata, and sees no harm in conspiring with the ruling classes against those classes 'in the middle'. This is the root of the 'conspiracy of evil' that arises from the libidinal economy of most class societies, and it becomes the wellspring of all dirty deals between this class and the more Machiavellian elements of the ruling class(es), from Caesarism to contemporary populism.

knowledge that they will self-destruct anyway, because during this self-destruction, they will also lay waste to everything that comes near them.

Is a 'Left' Populism Possible?

It is perfectly possible, as long as we unquestioningly accept the unsubstantiated claim that there *is* something to be called 'the Left' in the first place. After all, it is us who dumped together everything that included an ounce of oppositionality (and sometimes not even that), and called it 'the Left'. Communists and communalists, socialists and Fabians, trade-unionists and ecologists, feminists and queer activists, national liberationists and anti-imperialists, liberals and anarchists, social-democrats and plain democrats, the Bolsheviks and Turkish Kemalists, the Viet-Kong and the Khmer Rouge, Labour Party and the Communist Party of the Soviet Union, Spanish anarchists and communists of the Civil War and the Stalinists who massacred them, the German *Spartacusbund* of 1918 and the German Social Democrats who betrayed them and killed their leaders. They were all, at one time or another, included in this umbrella phrase, 'the Left'. Anybody who wanted to keep the pre-capitalistic element within modern capitalism was a conservative and belonged to 'the Right'. Anybody who opted for change, however small and insignificant, was on 'the Left'. Of course, time and again, this 'change' included corporatist measures, blatant statism, nationalism disguised as patriotism and/or anti-imperialism, Keynesianism, liberalism, and even at one time, in 1920's Italy, fascism. Everything was haphazardly stuffed together in this shapeless sack (not unlike the one in Buñuel's *Cet obscur objet du désir*), as long as the deadly calm imposed by a seemingly eternal capitalism held fast.

At the risk of (seeming to be) repeating myself, I will again say: ~~La~~ *[gauche] n'existe pas*: There is no such thing as '~~the~~ Left'. Consequently, when we set out to talk about, hypothesise, or even invent a 'Left Populism', we are merely referring to *an inexistence predicated upon a non-existence*, very much like Italo Calvino's *Il Cavaliere Inesistente*: the story of an empty full-plate armour, animated only by the dead knight's undying loyalty to his king. The People *as such* does not exist: it is an illusion, a fiction predicated upon a disregard of many actual elements that make up a population—social classes, genders, races, ethnicities, sexual orientations and ideological alignments; a handy universal to ignore a multiplicity of actual agencies in order to invent a single illusory agency which cannot speak for itself (since it *does not exist*), so it has to be *spoken for* by somebody else, an actual political agent, in our case, the populists. The Left *as such* also does not exist: it is a made-up category, a fiction predicated upon a disregard of many actual elements that supposedly make up a nebulous tendency for any kind of change or an un- (or ill-)defined 'progress'. Bring the two together, as 'Left Populism', and you have an impossible oxymoron, an untenable politico-ideological position, which can only serve, in the long run, the same populist agenda as the so-called 'Right Populism', only with a seemingly more 'radical' and/or liberating/liberal[25] rhetoric.

One of the most outstanding proponents of 'Left Populism', Chantal Mouffe, is quite forthcoming in her promotion of this idea (and prospective movement), that she sees 'the people' as 'a new subject of collective action':

> In his book *On Populist Reason*, Laclau defines populism as a discursive strategy of constructing a political frontier dividing society into two camps and calling for the mobilization of the 'underdog' against 'those in power'. [...] We can speak of a 'populist moment' when, under the pressure of political or socioeconomic transformations, the dominant hegemony is being destabilised by the multiplication of unsatisfied demands. In such situations, the existing institutions fail to secure the allegiance of the people as they attempt to defend the existing order. As a result, the historical bloc that provides the social basis of a hegemonic formation is being disarticulated and *the possibility arises of constructing a new subject of collective action – the people* – capable of reconfiguring a social order experienced as unjust. (Mouffe 2018, 20, my italics)

The first problem with this argument is not ideological or even political; it is historical: 'The People' is definitely not, nor can it be constru(ct)ed as, a '*new* subject'; it has *always* been 'the subject of collective action', that is, it was subjectivised as an illusory, fictional agent whenever the need for such an agent arose: an agent that did not exist in actuality, a spectre almost always invoked by the ruling classes whenever a need for the legitimation of non- or extra-legal measures arose. What Mouffe seems to miss in her analysis is the historical continuity of 'the People', as it is narratively represented in proto- and properly populist ideologies, from Caesarism to contemporary populism, and therefore her endeavour to present it as something *brand new*, something fresh and shiny that the beaten and tired 'Left' can pick up and use for its own purposes, is mostly in vain.

The second problem with Mouffe's argument is in her definition (which she attributes to Laclau): the definition of populism as a 'discursive strategy' (no problem so far), dividing society into two camps as 'the "underdog" against "those in power",' is a reiteration of the dimorphic logic we see Mouffe usually and Laclau sometimes, albeit seldom, employ. It is definitely possible to see society divided into two camps in revolutionary *moments*, as Marx and Engels did in 1848 ('the party of the revolution' vs. 'the party of order'), but this is limited to *moments* rather than periods or entire eras. Even then, the dimorphic structure is temporary and highly unstable, again, as it happened in 1848, when the 'party of the revolution' quickly split and disintegrated, and a more stable, trimorphic structure replaced it. The 'underdog' seldom evolves into a 'party of

---

[25] Although using the adjectives 'radical' and 'liberal' for the same noun seemingly creates an oxymoron, we should remember that we are already trying to describe an oxymoron.

the revolution' in and of itself as it is willy-nilly politicised, but is split between the two parties, the *lumpenproletariat* and the petty bourgeoisie usually going one way and the rest another. And this is only true for the 19th century Europe; in the 20th and 21st centuries things get immensely more complicated and the politicisation of social classes take many different forms, hitherto unimaginable coalitions and alliances arise and are broken, and although the basic class structure remains more or less intact, its representation in the political sphere resemble something completely bizarre and uncanny. In short, therefore, there is no shortcut from the 'underdog' to the 'party of the revolution'.

Likewise, no such shortcut exists from 'those in power' to the 'party of order', the ruling class, the dominant class or the governing class; to those who control the means of material and intellectual production, and those who control the circulation and dissemination of capital, commodities and knowledge. Although in the long-run of the Capitalist World-System, these can be seen as different aspects of a comprehensive single entity, in given historical moments they are different and often conflicting and incompatible subjects. Mouffe's dimorphic logic does not allow for this diversity, and treats both the 'underdog' and 'those in power' as integral subjects in and of themselves, which substitutes a *wish* for a concrete analysis of the facts of every specific era (including ours).

When we try to combine 'populism', therefore, predicated upon an imaginary subject, with 'the Left', at best an umbrella term which means little, if anything, under today's circumstances, we revive what is worst in both of them: a series of manipulations, demagoguery, self-victimisation, and a history of false representations unerringly ending up in empire. Furthermore (and worse), we also revive a political culture trying to squeeze Machiavellianism, naïve liberalism, statism disguised as collectivism, Social Democracy, Stalinism, and nationalism disguised as anti-imperialism, together in a carryall, assimilating and subverting radical anti-capitalism, that is, the collective endeavour to imagine a post-capitalist future still in its birth-throes. Alas, the concept of 'the People' is as beaten and tired as the 'Left' today, and no fusion of the two will provide us with something new, a movement that can weather the present profound crisis of neoliberalism, as the embodiment of the crisis of capitalism as a whole. One 'must be cruel, only to be kind': both 'the People' and 'the Left' are dead as useful analytical concepts, and the least we can do for them (in memory of the unforgettable Chilean slogan '*El pueblo, unido, jamás será vencido!*', or of the early *Montagnards* who sat on the 'Left' in the first really revolutionary assembly) is to give them a decent burial. Otherwise, like every dead body that is not properly buried, they will always return to haunt us.

Whither the 'Left'?

All these, however, are not the worst we can expect from a 'Left Populism':

119

the worst characteristic of populism (right *or* left) appears when 'the people' (or rather, the wolf pack hiding among the flock, the *lumpenproletariat*) demands its pound of flesh, so to speak, namely, a social class or stratum that exists, and should by all means remain, hierarchically on a lower plane than itself. Under today's circumstances, this class or stratum can be nothing but the mass of immigrants, who are moving with increasing speed among the third-world countries at war with each other and/or within themselves, and trying to reach Europe, the US, Canada, Australia and New Zealand at any cost.

A perfect example of this is visible in today's Turkey, which seems to have become a(n un)safe haven for immigrants mostly from Syria (the number is estimated between 3,5 and 4 million people), trying to reach Europe but stuck there for a purportedly temporary but actually indefinite period. The immigrants in Turkey are despised and demeaned by various sections of society, economically and culturally excluded, but at the same time exploited as an illegal and cheap labour force and more often than not, as sexual objects: their women are driven into prostitution and/or into becoming 'second wives' for wealthy Turkish men, and their children are under constant threat of abuse and rape. On top of this, the AKP government uses them as a bargaining chip, threatening the EU to 'open its borders' if the EU does not provide free funding (supposedly for the immigrants) and support for its ongoing (un?)declared war against the Kurdish elements in Northern Syria. The immigrants, therefore, are unwanted and subject to xenophobia and racist attacks, but still maintained to form a yet lower echelon in society, upon which 'the people' may have an illusory domination.

Populism, no matter however 'left' of 'good-intentioned', cannot resist this immense pressure to keep the immigrants at the lowest rung of the food chain, which seems to be coming from 'the people', but actually is a result of different sections of the population being manipulated by the *lumpenproletariat* already in cohorts with the shrewdest elements within the ruling class. This entails, first, keeping the immigrants in a state of nebulous legal uncertainty. Secondly, immigrants, in case that they are not immediately deported or 'kept out', should provide (a) a cheap labour force; and (b) an *objet petit a*, an object of both desire and abjection. Any political ideology and/or movement that defines its 'base' as an imaginary 'people', supposedly regardless of class, gender or race, in fact 'represents' a hidden kernel in this nebulous quasi-subject, in most cases the *lumpenproletariat* sanctioned by the ruling class(es). Any 'left' attempt at populism – 'left' loosely meaning any egalitarian and/or libertarian political ideology that strives for a post-capitalist future in this case— cannot escape the real material drive that resides within the illusory 'people'. When Mouffe suggests establishing 'a chain of equivalence among the demands of the workers, the immigrants and the precarious middle class,' therefore, she is not only demanding the *impossible*, which can be something revolutionary, but also the *improbable*:

Left populism on the contrary wants to recover democracy to deepen and extend it. A left populist strategy aims at federating the democratic demands into a collective will to construct a 'we', a 'people' confronting a common adversary: the oligarchy. This requires the establishment of a chain of equivalence among the demands of the workers, the immigrants and the precarious middle class, as well as other democratic demands, such as those of the LGBT community. The objective of such a chain is the creation of a new hegemony that will permit the radicalization of democracy. (Mouffe 2018, 24)

In her haste 'to construct a "we", a "people"' against the 'oligarchy', a 'people' which apparently *includes* the immigrants, Mouffe overlooks the fact that we first have to *deconstruct* the 'people' already in circulation, fabricated by the existing populists, the one which is predicated *against* the immigrants. In doing so, we must necessarily deconstruct the narrative of populism as well, because once this 'people' is gone, populism will have nothing to represent and consequently become immediately obsolete. In other words, it is impossible to extract the working class and 'the precarious middle class' from that classless hotchpotch called the 'people', that 'subject which is not a subject', that ageless inamorata of all ruling classes throughout written history, without conceptually dismantling it first in its entirety.

It is possible to understand the difficulty to resist the appeal (indeed the *lure*) of populism for those who are critical –or, to be blunt, sick and tired— of the inherent elitism of many so-called 'leftist' ideologies and positions, but, alas, populism is not the cure: it is rather an inseparable part of the ailment. As long as we insist on thinking in terms of the populist/elitist or underdog/elite dichotomies, we will necessarily miss the fact that without an *Aufhebung* of that plane of argument we will end up where we begin. Populism and elitism are not only two equally soiled ends of the same stick; they *are* the same stick: every so-called populist ideology and/or movement not only invents a 'people' so that it can speak for it, it also, as a part of the same act, distances itself from its own creation and hierarchically places itself above it. It is not a coincidence that almost every populist or proto-populist ideology in Turkey, from the pan-Turkic early opposition to the Ottoman Sultanate, to many allegedly socialist groups of the 60s and 70s, and in some cases even of today, uses the same catch-phrase 'to *go down* to the people' ('*halka inmek*').

It is an inevitable fundamental rule of every binary hierarchical social structure, however, that the dimorphic construction of society necessarily creates a third, making it a triune structure. The third, the 'other' which seemingly unites the other two so that the hierarchic interrelation between them could be blurred, opacified and eventually ignored, has taken on various forms. This 'third other' has almost always been *women* throughout history and across various social formations; it can be the *slaves* (or ex-slaves) in specific social formations (Greek, Roman and Colonial American), and it is, like women, almost always the *foreigners*, not only as an external threat, as outsiders, but also as an internal element, from the Ancient Greek *metoikoi* to today's immigrants and asylum-seekers. It will be an exceedingly optimistic attitude to claim that when 'the left' dons the mantle of populism, it may be able to escape the urge to create and debase this 'third other', which is how populism manages and manipulates the 'people', using the prejudices among its most despicable elements. We must keep in mind that whenever a libertarian and/or egalitarian political entity has spoken in favour of immigrants, as in German Green Party's early 80s slogan '*Ich bin ein Ausländer!*', it is almost always from a non- (or even anti-) populist position.[26] Consequently, as *Die Grüne* became more and more of an establishment party, it dropped the radical *pro-Ausländer* position, and although it never became anti-immigration *per se*, incorporating many (but mostly assimilated) immigrants in its ranks, it did not return to the radical position of the 80s.

The 'left' has always tended towards sexism, homophobia, racism and xenophobia, *not structurally*, not as an ideological prerogative, but only when it tried to employ populist strategies, and has done this usually semi-knowingly, putting the blame on the 'people', the allegedly uneducated, moralistic, traditionalistic and 'innately' conservative and even reactionary mass it allegedly represents. It always has remained in the clear, owning up to none of these characteristics: eventually, however, it *becomes all of these* in the middle-run, while the 'people', not being an actual, integrated subject, is none. There have always been sexist, homophobic, racist and xenophobic elements *within* the 'people', but whether (any of) these elements will become dominant is subject to a continuing, almost never-ending struggle, as an integral part of the already ongoing class struggle. Sexism, homophobia, racism and xenophobia have always been the 'ideas of the ruling class':

> The ideas of the ruling class are in every epoch the ruling ideas: i.e., the class which is the ruling material force of society is at the same time its ruling intellectual force. The class which has the means of material production at its disposal, consequently also controls the means of mental production, so that the ideas of those who lack the means of mental production are on the whole subject to it. [...] Insofar, therefore, as they rule as a class and determine the extent and compass of an historical epoch, it is self-evident that they do this in its whole range, hence among other things rule also as thinkers, as producers of ideas, and regulate the production and distribution of the ideas of their age: thus, their ideas are the ruling ideas of the epoch. (Marx & Engels 1998, 67)

---

[26] It is interesting to note that the slogan '*Ich bin ein Ausländer!*' which was an integral part of the German Green Party's immigration policy in the 1980's, has almost entirely been erased from popular memory. When you try googling the slogan, the only thing you get is the song of the same name by the 80s and 90s alternative rock band, Pop will Eat Itself.

No matter how well-intentioned or libertarian/egalitarian the 'left populists' may be, the moment they opt for 'representing the people' as it stands as a unified subject, rather than already infinitely divided by class struggle, they necessarily take over the current dominant ideas of the 'entire' people, which are the dominant ideas, that is, the ideological prejudices, of the ruling class. In order to avoid this fate, they have to subvert the presumed unity of the 'people', and acknowledge its fragmented/conflicted structure and the ongoing class struggle within, thereby disowning the 'populist' epithet they adopted in the first place. This move will probably create an ambiguity about the possible outcome of the struggle, an unpredictability which most 'left' political movements and ideologies dread and abhor, after decades, indeed centuries, of (sometimes humiliating) defeats. The ambiguity and unpredictability, however, are precisely what a truly libertarian/egalitarian (or using Balibar's neologism once more, 'equalibertarian' [Balibar 2014]) political movement needs. Unpredictability causes, according to Wallerstein, 'confusion, anger, disparagement of those in power, and above all acute fear', not only in the left, but also in the ruling class itself:

> The basic reality is unpredictability not merely in some middle run but very much in the short run. The sociopsychological consequences of this short-run unpredictability have been confusion, anger, disparagement of those in power, and above all acute fear. This fear leads to the search for political alternatives of kinds not entertained before. The media refer to this as populism, but it is far more complicated than this slogan term suggests. For some the fear leads to multiple and irrational scapegoatings. For others, it leads to the willingness to unthink deeply ingrained assumptions about the operations of the modern world-system. This can be seen in the United States as the difference between the Tea Party movement and the Occupy Wall Street movement. (Wallerstein 2013, 32)

The desperate need for absolute clarity and predictability has been haunting the 'left' almost for centuries now, and has even given rise to an almost blind faith in positivism, which has been discredited over and over again, not only in social sciences and humanities, but also in 'hard' sciences themselves, starting as early as 1927, with Heisenberg's Uncertainty Principle:

> But what is wrong in the sharp formulation of the law of causality, 'When we know the present precisely, we can predict the future,' is not the conclusion but the assumption. Even in principle we cannot know the present in all detail. (Heisenberg 1983, 83).

The pursuit for a poor certainty and predictability among socialists and communists (even among anarchists) is a gloomy outcome of the years following the 'defeat' of the traditional anti-systemic movements in the 1990s, which caused a wide-ranging confusion, disarray, disorientation and a sense of panic in the 'left' in general. Decades (almost centuries) of setbacks and the consequent descent into insignificance and feeling of impotence had already created in the radical anti-capitalist camp a need to *hide*, among or within more mainstream political entities, and the indefinite and nebulous concept of the 'left' was a perfect hiding place for such an escape: hence the insistence on the term, 'left', although everybody is surreptitiously aware that it is analytically hollow.

As the traditional, institutionalised 'left' disintegrated, however, and even the social democratic parties with a more or less socialist (even Marxist) past were entrenched more and more in the neoliberal establishment, it became harder and harder to 'hide'. The concept of 'Left' populism offers us one of the more recent recesses to go on hiding, trying to mimic what we perceive as the '*vox populi*', but is, in fact, the discourse of the ruling class, disguised as 'public opinion', using the rhetoric of the *lumpenproletariat*. We become 'mottled against a mottled background', as Homi Bhabha quotes Lacan in his 'Of Mimicry and Men'[27] (Bhabha 1994, 85), and one day we wake up, not much unlike Kafka's cockroach, to find ourselves to have become nothing but mottles.

The ability to imagine a non-capitalist future has its own language and style, something not inherently elitist or arrogant, something anybody (belonging to 'the people') without a secondary (or indeed primary) benefit in things remaining as they are, can understand, join in and enjoy. Decades of 'defeats' and the resentment thereof, often against the 'people' who refused to 'follow' us while we were suffering *for* them, may have made us forget this language, and driven us to mimic others, liberals, social-democrats, authoritarian and totalitarian leaders, sometimes even fascists, and now the populists, in the hope of snatching victory while, like Odysseus, in disguise. Every time we do this, however, we become a little more *like* them. We need to see clearly that this consistent mimicry hasn't brought us victory, not even the faintest semblance of it, but only changed us and made us pale ghosts of what we are mimicking. What we need is to find (again) our own language, our own voice, not above 'the people', not mimicking the self-appointed 'representatives' of 'the people', but only, as Marx and Engels had pointed out in 1848, '[to] express, in general terms, actual relations springing from an existing class struggle, from a historical movement going on under our very eyes.' (Marx & Engels 2010)

---

[27] The quotation is from Lacan's 'Of the Gaze' in *Four Fundamental Concepts of Psychoanalysis*:
Mimicry reveals something in so far as it is distinct from what might be called an itself that is behind. The effect of mimicry is camouflage [...] It is not a question of harmonizing with the background, but against a mottled background, of becoming mottled - exactly like the technique of camouflage practised in human warfare. (Lacan 1998, 99)

Bibliography

Anderson, Benedict (2006). Imagined Communities Reflections on the Origin and Spread of Nationalism. London & New York: Verso.

Bal, Mieke (2018). 'Let's Abolish the Peer-Review System' in *Media Theory* 23.

Balibar, Etienne (2014). *Equaliberty: Political Essays*. Tr. James Ingram. Durham: Duke University Press.

Barthes, Roland (1974). *S/Z*. Tr. Richard Miller. New York: Hill & Wang.

Bell, Kirsten (2017). 'Predatory' Open Access Journals as Parody: Exposing the Limitations of 'Legitimate' Academic Publishing; *tripleC* 15(2): 651-662, 2017, http://www.triple-c.at.

Bernasconi, Robert (ed.) (2001). *Concepts of Race in the Eighteenth Century* (8 volumes). Bristol: Thoemmes.

Berry, David M. and Giles Moss (eds). (2008). *Libre Culture: Meditations on Free Culture*; Winnipeg: Pygmalion Books.

Bhabha, Homi (1990). 'DissemiNation: Time, Narrative, and the Margins of the Modern Nation'; in Homi Bhabha (ed.) *Nation and Narration*, 291-322. New York: Routledge.

Bhabha, Homi (1994). 'Of Mimicry and Man'; in *The Location of Culture*, 85-92. New York: Routledge.

Biswas, Asit K. & Julian Kirchherr (2015). 'Prof, no one is reading you'; in *The Straits Times*, 11 April 2015.

Bloch, Ernst (1996). *The Principle of Hope*. Vol. 1. Tr. Neville Plaice, Stephen Plaice and Paul Knight. Cambridge, MA: The MIT Press.

Bolton, John (2020). *The Room Where It Happened: A White House Memoir*. New York: Simon & Schuster.

Bracher, Mark (1993). Lacan, Discourse, and Social Change: A Psychoanalytic Cultural Criticism. Ithaca and London: Cornell University Press.

Brecht, Bertolt (1963). *Leben des Galilei*; Berlin: Suhrkamp Verlag AG.

Brecht, Bertolt (1995). *Life of Galileo*; in *Brecht: Collected Plays*, vol. 5. Tr. John Willett. London: Bloomsbury.

Busch, Lawrence (2017). Knowledge for Sale: The Neoliberal Takeover of Higher Education. Boston: The MIT Press.

Canovan, Margaret (1999). 'Trust the People! Populism and the Two Faces of Democracy'; in *Political Studies* (1999), XLVII, 2-16.

Carroll, Lewis (1999). *The Annotated Alice: The Definitive Edition*. NY & London: W. W. Norton & Co.

Çavdar, Ayşe (2018). 'The State (of Mind) of Dumrul: How did a Nation Lose the Plot?'; in *Freie Assoziation*; 21. Jahrgang 2/2018, 40-60.

Chatterjee, Partha (1986). Nationalist Thought and the Colonial World: A Derivative Discourse. London: Zed Books.

de Beauvoir, Simone (1949). Ethics of Ambiguity. Tr. Bernard Frechtman. https://www.marxists.org/reference/subject/ethics/de-beauvoir/ambiguity/

Dean, Jodi (2009). Democracy and Other Neoliberal Fantasies: Communicative Capitalism & Left Politics. Durham & London: Duke University Press.

Derrida, Jacques (1991). *Given Time: 1. Counterfeit Money*. Tr. Peggy Kamouf. Chicago and London: Chicago University Press.

Dostoevsky, Fyodor (1991). *The Brothers Karamazov*. Tr. Richard Pevear and Larissa Volokhonsky. New York: Vintage Classics.

Emerson, Ralph Waldo (2004). *Essays*. Coradella Collegiate Bookshelf Editions.

Engels Frederick (2010). *The Peasant War in Germany*; in Marx & Engels, *Collected Works, Vol. 10.* London: Lawrence and Wishart.

Engels Frederick (2010). 'Preface to the Second Edition of *The Peasant War in Germany*'; in Marx & Engels, *Collected Works, Vol. 21.* London: Lawrence and Wishart.

Finchelstein, Federico (2017). *From Fascism to Populism in History.* Oakland, CA: University of California Press.

Flexner, Abraham (1939). 'The Usefulness of Useless Knowledge'; in *Harpers,* issue 179, June/November 1939.

Foucault, Michel (1977). '*La fonction politique de l'intellectuel*', in *Dits et écrits, vol. II: 1976–1988,* eds. D. Defert and F. Ewald, Paris: Gallimard, 2001, 109–114. English translation (a shorter version) by Colin Gordon; 'The Political Function of the Intellectual', in *Radical Philosophy, 17 (Summer 1977),* 12–14.

Foucault, Michel (1983). 'The Subject and Power', in Hubert L. Dreyfus and Paul Rabinow (eds), *Michel Foucault: Beyond Structuralism and Hermeneutics*; Chicago: The University of Chicago Press.

Foucault, Michel (1995). *Discipline and Punish: The Birth of the Prison.* New York: Vintage Books.

Foucault, Michel (2001). *Fearless Speech.* Ed. Joseph Pearson. Los Angeles, CA: Semiotext(e).

Foucault, Michel (2008). *The Birth of Biopolitics: Lectures at the Collège de France, 1978–79.* Ed. Michel Senellart. London: Palgrave Macmillan.

Foucault, Michel (2009). *Security, Territory, Population: Lectures at the Collège de France, 1977–78.* Ed. Michel Senellart. London: Palgrave Macmillan.

Freud, Sigmund, 2001. *Totem and Taboo.* NY & London: Routledge.

Greenberg, Daniel S. (2007). *Science for Sale: The Perils, Rewards, and Delusions of Campus Capitalism.* Chicago and London: The University of Chicago Press.

Gunder Frank, Andre (1972*). Lumpenbourgeoisie Lumpendevelopment: Dependence, Class, and Politics in Latin America.* Tr. Marion Davis Berdecio. New York & London: Monthly Review Press.

Guy, Simon (2019). 'The hollowing out of Game of Thrones'. Socialist Review; http://socialist review.org.uk/447/hollowing-out-game-thrones).

Hawkins, Kirk A., Cristóbal Rovira Kaltwasser and Ioannis Andreadis (2018). 'The Activation of Populist Attitudes*'; Government and Opposition* (2018), 0, 1–25

Hawkins, Kirk A., Ryan E. Carlin, Levente Littvay, and Cristóbal Rovira Kaltwasser, eds. (2019). *The Ideational Approach to Populism: Concept, Theory, and Analysis.* London & New York: Routledge.

Heisenberg, Werner (1969). *Der Teil und das Ganze,* Tr. G. Holton. Munich: R. Piper & Co.

Heisenberg, Werner (1983 [1927]). "The Uncertainty Paper", in *Quantum Theory and Measurement,* 62-86. Eds. John Archibald Wheeler & Wojciech Hubert Zurek; Princeton, NJ: Princeton University Press.

Holquist, Michael & Robert Shulman, George Levine, M. Norton Wise, Nina Byers, et al. (1996). 'Sokal's Hoax: An Exchange'; in *The New York Review of Books* October 3, 1996.

Horowitz, Jason (2018). 'Steve Bannon Is Done Wrecking the American Establishment. Now He Wants to Destroy Europe's'. *The New York Times,* March 9, 2018.

Hyland, Ken (2015). Academic Publishing: Issues and Challenges in the Construction of Knowledge. Oxford: Oxford University Press.

Iglesias Turrión, Pablo (2014). 'Pesentación' in Pablo Iglesias Turrión (ed.), *Ganar o morir: Lecciones políticas en Juego de Tronos* (Win or Die: Political Lessons from The Game of Thrones). Madrid: Ediciónes Akal.

Jalava, Jarkko, Stephanie Griffiths, and Michael Maraun (2015). *The Myth of the Born Criminal: Psychopathy, Neurobiology, and the Creation of the Modern Degenerate.* Toronto: University of Toronto Press.

Kant, Immanuel (1887). The Philosophy of Law: An Exposition of the Fundamental Principles of Jurisprudence as the Science of Right; trans. W. Hastie, Edinburgh: Clark.

Kant, Immanuel (2006). 'An Answer to the Question: What Is Enlightenment?'; in *Toward Perpetual Peace and Other Writings on Politics, Peace, and History;* Ed. Pauline Kleingeld, Tr. David L. Colclasure. New Haven and London: Yale University Press; 17-23.

Kofman, Ava (2018). 'Bruno Latour, the Post-Truth Philosopher, Mounts a Defense of Science' in *The New York Times Magazine,* Oct. 25, 2018. https://www.nytimes.com/2018/10/25/magazine/bruno-latour-post-truth-philosopher-science.html.

Kwon, Diana (2019). 'Elsevier and Norway Agree on New Open-Access Deal'; in The Scientist, April 24, 2019. https://www.the-scientist.com/news-opinion/elsevier-and-norway-agree-on-new-open-access-deal-65789.

Lacan, Jacques (2007). *The Seminar of Jacques Lacan, Book XVII: The Other Side of Psychoanalysis.* Ed. Jacques-Alain Miller, Tr. Russell Grigg. New York & London: W. W. Norton & Company.

Laclau, Ernesto (2005). *On Populist Reason.* London & New York: Verso.

Latour, Bruno (2004). 'Why Has Critique Run out of Steam? From Matters of Fact to Matters of Concern'; in *Critical Inquiry,* Vol. 30, No. 2 (Winter 2004), 225-248.

Le Guin, Ursula (1993). 'Stalin in the Soul', in *The Language of the Night.* New York: Harper & Collins.

Le Guin, Ursula (2014), *National Book Award Acceptance Speech.* http://www.sfcenter.ku.edu/LeGuin- NBA-Medalist-Speech.htm.

Lorenz, Chris (2012). 'If You're So Smart, Why Are You under Surveillance? Universities, Neoliberalism, and New Public Management', in *Critical Inquiry* 38 (Spring 2012).

Marx, Karl (1843 [2010a]). 'Letter to Ruge'; in *Collected Works, Vol. III.* London: Lawrence & Wishart.

Marx, Karl & Frederick Engels (1845 [1998]). *The   German Ideology.* New York: Prometheus Books.

Marx, Karl & Frederick Engels (1848 [2010b]). *The   Communist Manifesto,* in *Collected Works, Vol. VI.* London: Lawrence & Wishart.

Marx, Karl (1852 [1960]). *Der achtzehnte Brumaire des Louis Bonaparte.* In Marx & Engels, *Werke Band 8.* Berlin: Dietz Verlag.

Marx, Karl (1852 [2010c]). The Eighteenth Brumaire of Louis Bonaparte, in Collected Works, Vol. XI. London: Lawrence & Wishart.

Marx, Karl (1857-58 [1964]). *Pre-Capitalist Economic Formations.* New York, New York: International Publishers.

Marx, Karl (1859 [1999]). *A Contribution to the Critique of Political Economy.* Moscow: Progress Publishers.

Marx, Karl (1862-63 [1969]). *Theories of Surplus Value: Part I.* Moscow: Progress Publishers.

Michael, Hagner (2018). 'Open Access, Data Capitalism and Academic Publishing', in *Swiss Med Wkly.* 2018; 148: w14600.

Mouffe, Chantal (2018). *For a Left Populism.* London & New York: Verso.

Moyers, Bill D (1988). 'What a Real President was Like'. *The Washington Post,* November 13, 1988.

Mudde, Cas and Cristóbal Rovira Kaltwasser (2017). *Populism: A Very Short Introduction.* Oxford & New York: Oxford University Press.

Nietzsche, Friedrich (1974). *The Gay Science.* Tr. Walter Kaufmann. New York: Vintage Books.

Nietzsche, Friedrich (1989). *On the Genealogy of Morals* and *Ecce Homo.* Tr. Walter Kaufman & R. J. Hollingdale; ed. Walter Kaufman. New York: Vintage Books.

Ordine, Nuccio (2017). *The Usefulness of the Useless.* Tr. Alastair McEwen. Philadelphia: Paul Dry Books.

Özkırımlı, Umut (2000). *Theories of Nationalism: A Critical Introduction.* Hampshire: Palgrave

Macmillan.

Özkırımlı, Umut (2005). Contemporary Debates on Nationalism: A Critical Engagement. Hampshire: Palgrave Macmillan.

Parker, Ian (2014). 'Negotiating text with Lacan: theory into practice' in Ian Parker and David Pavón-Cuéllar, eds.; *Lacan, Discourse, Event: New Psychoanalytic Approaches to Textual Indeterminacy*. London & NY: Routledge, 52-65.

Pozzo, Riccardo (2006). 'Immanuel Kant on Intellectual Property'; in *Trans/Form/Ação*, São Paulo, 29(2): 11-18.

Raskolnikov, F. F. (1934). 'The Tale of a Lost Day'; in *Tales of Sub-Lieutenant Ilyin*: https://www. marxists.org/history/ussr/government/red-army/1918/raskolnikov/ilyin/index.htm.

Raunig, Gerald (2013). Factories of Knowledge, Industries of Creativity. Los Angeles: Semiotext(e).

Rovira Kaltwasser, Cristóbal, Paul Taggart Paulina Ochoa Espejo & Pierre Ostiguy, eds. (2018). *The Oxford Handbook of Populism*. Oxford & New York: Oxford University Press.

Salecl, Renata (1994). 'Deference to the Great Other: The Discourse of Education', in Bracher, Max, et. al.; *Lacanian Theory of Discourse: Subject, Structure, and Society*. New York and London: New York University Press.

Smith, Richard (2006). 'Peer review: a flawed process at the heart of science and Journals', in *Journal of the Royal Society of Medicine* Volume 99 April 2006.

Sokal, Alan and Jean Bricmont (1998). Fashionable Nonsense: Postmodern Intellectuals' Abuse of Science. New York: Picador.

Somay, Bülent (2010). The View from the Masthead: Journey through Dystopia towards and Open-Ended Utopia. Istanbul: Istanbul Bilgi University Press.

Staley, David (2019). Alternative Universities: Speculative Design for Innovation in Higher Education. Baltimore: Johns Hopkins University Press.

Spivak, Gayatri Chakravorty (2009). 'They the people: Problems of Alter-globalization'; in *Radical Philosophy157* (September/October 2009), 31-36.

Strauss, David A. (2013). 'We the People, They the People, and the Puzzle of Democratic Constitutionalism'; in *Texas Law Review* [Vol. 91:1969 2013], 1969-1981.

Swartz, Aaron (2008). 'Guerilla Open Access Manifesto'; https://archive.org/stream/Guerilla OpenAccessManifesto/Goamjuly2008_djvu.txt.

Thalheimer, August (1930). 'On Fascism'. From What's Next magazine. https://marxists. architexturez. net/ archive/thalheimer/works/fascism.htm.

Tirelli, Vincent (2014). 'Contingent Academic Labor Against Neoliberalism'; in *New Political Science*, 36:4, 523-537, DOI: 10.1080/07393148.2014.954791.

The Editors of Lingua Franca (2000). *The Sokal Hoax: The Sham that Shook the Academy*. Lincoln and London: University of Nebraska Press

Tirelli, Vincent (2014). 'Contingent Academic Labor Against Neoliberalism'; in *New Political Science*, 36:4, 523-537, DOI: 10.1080/07393148.2014.954791.

Trotsky, Leon (1934). 'Bonapartism and Fascism'; in *New International*, Vol.1 No.2, August 1934, 37-38.

Tüfekçi, Zeynep (2019). 'The Real Reason Fans Hate the Last Season of Game of Thrones'. Scientific American, https://blogs.scientificamerican.com/observations/the-real-reason-fans-hate-the-last-season-of-game-of-thrones/?redirect=1).

Urbinati, Nadia (2013). 'The Populist Phenomenon'; in *Presses de Sciences Po «Raisons politiques»*, 2013/3 N° 51; 137-154.

Verhaeghe, Paul (1995). "From Impossibility to Inability: Lacan's Theory of the Four Discourses"; in *The Letter* (Dublin).

Wade, Mark and Michael Mabe (2015). *The STM Report: An Overview of Scientific and Scholarly Journal*

Publishing; Fourth Edition. https://www.stm-assoc.org/2015_02_20_STM_ Report_2015.pdf.

Wallerstein, Immanuel (1992). 'The Collapse of Liberalism'; in *The Socialist Register*, vol. 28.

Wallerstein, Immanuel (1995). *After Liberalism*. New York: The New Press.

Wallerstein, Immanuel (1999). *The End of the World as We Know It: Social Science for the Twenty-First Century*. Minneapolis & London: University of Minnesota Press.

Wallerstein, Immanuel (2004A). *The Uncertainties of Knowledge*. Philadelphia: Temple University Press.

Wallerstein, Immanuel (2004B). *World-Systems Analysis: An Introduction*. Durham & London: Duke University Press.

Wallerstein, Immanuel (2006). *European Universalism: The Rhetoric of Power*. New York and London: The New Press.

Wallerstein, Immanuel (2013). 'Structural Crisis, or Why Capitalists May No Longer Find Capitalism Rewarding'; in Immanuel Wallerstein, Randall Collins, Michael Mann, Georgi Derluguian & Craig Calhoun, *Does Capitalism have a Future?* Oxford & New York: Oxford University Press.

Watt, Ian (1972). *The Rise of the Novel*; Harmondsworth: Pelican.

Zamyatin, Yevgeny (1970). 'On Literature, Revolution, Entropy, and Other Matters'; in *A Soviet Heretic: Essays by Yevgeny Zamyatin*. Ed. & trans. Mirra Ginsburg. Chicago & London: The University of Chicago Press.

Zitek, Emily M. Alexander H. Jordan, Benoit Monin, and Frederick R. Leach (2010), 'Victim Entitlement to Behave Selfishly'; in *Journal of Personality and Social Psychology*, 2010, Vol. 98, No. 2, 245–255.

Žižek, Slavoj (1998) 'A Leftist Plea for 'Eurocentrism'; in *Critical Inquiry*, Vol. 24, No. 4 (Summer, 1998), 988-1009.

Žižek, Slavoj (1999). 'Against the Double Blackmail'; in *Third Text*, 13:47, 39-50, DOI: 10.1080/09528829908576794.

Žižek, Slavoj (2003-4). "*L'homo sacer comme objet du discours de l'Université*", *Cités* 2003/4 (n° 16), p. 25-41. DOI 10.3917/cite.016.0025.

Žižek, Slavoj (2006). 'Jacques Lacan's Four Discourses'. http://www.lacan.com/zizfour.htm.

Žižek, Slavoj (2008). *In Defence of Lost Causes*; London: Verso.

Žižek, Slavoj (2019). 'Game of Thrones tapped into fears of revolution and political women – and left us no better off than before'. The Independent, https://www.independent.co.uk/ voices/ game-thrones-season-8-finale-bran-daenerys-cersei-jon-snow-zizek-revolution-a892 3371.html).

www.ingramcontent.com/pod-product-compliance
Lightning Source LLC
Chambersburg PA
CBHW030852270326
41928CB00008B/1334